This book is
dedicated to you

{for Mum R.I.P}

**Open manifesto:
Enlightened Self-interest**

This issue:

Edited and designed by Kevin Finn.
Copy proofing by KT Doyle, Brisbane, Australia.
Copyright © 2015. The Sum Of Pty Ltd.
All rights reserved.

First edition published in Australia, 2015.
Printed by www.lulu.com

Design by Kevin Finn, The Sum Of.
Cover photograph Kevin Finn © The Sum Of.

Transcriptions by CastingWords.

All type set in Clarendon and Times New Roman Italic.
Headings in Clarendon Bold.
Text in Clarendon Light.
Emphasis in Times New Roman Italic (Bold and Light).

Open manifesto is produced and published independently by The Sum Of Pty Ltd.
Open manifesto can be reached at: www.openmanifesto.net

Though *Open manifesto* may not necessarily agree with everything it publishes, it does uphold the need and importance of debate. The individual nature of opinion reflects the dynamism, colour and distinct qualities that make up any vibrant community, and this should be universally encouraged.

ABN: 43-110-227-971
ISSN: 1832-5947
ISBN: 978-0-9944180-0-5

Open manifesto takes no responsibility and is not liable for inaccurate or false information contained in the contributors texts. While *Open manifesto* does all it's power to check information, contributions are solely the responsibility of the individual contributor and rely on the personal knowledge, research and experience of the contributor.

Preface / Introduction	02
Everything is connected Kevin Finn in conversation with Ji Lee	06
Give and Take Kevin Finn in conversation with Adam Grant	44
Thinking to create value Kevin Finn in conversation with Edward de Bono	68
The language of culture, happiness and hostility Kevin Finn in conversation with Dan Everett	82
The writing on the wall: **Notes from the field #5, London** An essay by Anne Miltenburg	104
Gangnam Style: **Notes from the field #4, Seoul** An essay by Anne Miltenburg	110
The community consequence of our creation An essay by Andrew Barnum	118
All our actions are interactions. An essay by Stephanie Akkaoui Hughes	130
No logos; No straplines; No slogans! Just culture Kevin Finn in conversation with Helen Palmer	146
Design. Brand. Business. Kevin Finn in conversation with Damian Borchok	178
Self-interest Exam for Graphic Designers An exercise by Jason A. Tselentis	220
Contributors biographies The people behind this issue	230
Back issues Information on previous issues	238
Thanks Acknowledgements by Kevin Finn	250

Preface / Introduction

This issue of Open Manifesto was largely inspired by a conversation I had in 2008 with the late, and legendary, Wally Olins [Open Manifesto #5]. It was while chatting with Wally that I first heard the phrase *Enlightened Self-interest*, which he used to describe how some organisations believe *"it will be in [their] interest to become charitable, or to be seen to become charitable—I don't want to sound cynical here but the appropriate phrase is 'enlightened self-interest'. If they see it as being in their interest to be socially responsible, then that is what they will do. And that is a very powerful mechanism for change."*

This sparked my interest to explore the topic further—and as widely as I could. After a far longer period than I had hoped, you are reading the result of this exploration.

Which brings me to an apology. For various personal reasons, which the contributors are aware of—and who have been incredibly supportive and understanding—I was unable to attend to Open Manifesto #7 for the better part of a year. For the following year, I had to work very hard to overcome those personal circumstances, and had even begun referring to Open Manifesto #7 as *the lost issue*. However, I am incredibly excited—and humbled—to finally bring issue #7 to you!

Once again, like previous issues I have handpicked each contributor for their insights, opinions and expertise, before presenting them in this single volume—a passion that I am incredibly fortunate to be able to pursue. And like previous issues I truly believe issue #7 has been worth taking the time to research, source, produce and collect each specific contribution—and I hope you'll agree.

As always, I owe a debt of gratitude to each contributor, for their patience and support—particularly those who submitted material at the beginning of the process. A lot of time has passed from my initial contact with many of the contributors.

Over the duration of this issue I have been reminded that life happens and, whether we are prepared or not, we face things we had never expected. Sometimes we are called to face the things we fear or dread. Many can be life-changing.

Life.*

*Available for a limited time only. Limit one (1) per person. Subject to change without notice. Provided "as is" and without any warranties. Nontransferable and is the sole responsibility of the recipient. May incur damages arising from use or misuse. Additional parts sold separately. Your mileage may vary. Subject to all fees and taxes. Terms and conditions apply. Other restrictions apply.

Annymous.
We tried very hard, but without success, to source the author of this writing.

As a result, over the past couple of years I have been constently reminded that we really only get once shot at life and that it's vital we don't to take it for granted.

You can probably tell this issue has a very personal significance for me. Aside from enduring various hurdles over the period of producing this issue, *enlightened self-interest* conveys much of what Open Manifesto is about. For me, *enlightened self-interest* means pursuing a personal interest—but where the result of this benefits many others.

From the outset I began Open Manifesto to expand my own knowledge and understanding of the world we live in, and how design and creativity relates to it. I have always sought to share this with as many people as I can—through the pages of Open Manifesto and through my various speaking engagements. My passion is to connect, with as many people as possible, the insights and opinions from some of the world's most compelling thought leaders.

After a decade—and seven issues—my passion hasn't ceased. And once again, each contributor has been incredibly generous, honest, insightful and inspirational.

Settle in, and enjoy!

Kevin Finn
Founder & Editor

Everything is connected

Kevin Finn in conversation with Ji Lee

Kevin Finn: It's clear your work is centered on ideas and much of it is driven by your personal interests. But an underlying objective also seems to be that other people can also interact or benefit from those particular projects. With this in mind, would it be fair to describe your personal work as an exercise in enlightened self-interest?

Ji Lee: Yes, I think so. However, *enlightened* is a big word. I don't claim there's any aspect of me that is particularly enlightened. I think the enlightened part is a process towards better understanding myself, and also trying to connect with other people through this process.

But you do get a lot more enjoyment when people do interact with the work that you're creating...

Absolutely!

So it's not just about your own growth and learning, and becoming more enlightened. Would you agree it's more about asking: *"How can others participate?"*

Yes. My process, which is often participatory, really wasn't something that I did consciously—it just sort of happened naturally. I think the first project where I fully realized the power of opening up for others to participate was *The Bubble Project*, which probably goes back ten years. It happened when I was working at *Saatchi & Saatchi*.

I studied graphic design, but I originally came to New York to study fine arts. That was my goal. As a child I always wanted to become a painter—Picasso and Van Gogh, those were my childhood idols. I always liked to draw and paint and my parents were always supportive of what I did, in terms of artistic activities.

Then, with the support of my parents, I came to New York to study fine arts. The first year consisted of studying general liberal arts. In my second year I chose fine arts as my major. I did the first semester and I realized that fine arts really wasn't that interesting because the education of fine arts in my school, and I think generally speaking, is very theoretical—a lot of discussion; it's less practical and more theoretical.

I didn't really feel inspired by the teachers. In fact, I felt they were sort of unsuccessful, frustrated artists themselves. I saw that a lot of students, who graduated from the fine arts department, didn't actually become successful artists. They were either waiting tables or becoming construction workers. They were really struggling financially and artistically. In the end, a lot of them simply gave up in order to pursue something else. That didn't encourage me.

I switched my major to graphic design because I saw a lot of interesting projects coming from the graphic design department and quickly fell in love with it. I really liked the fact that graphic design had very artistic aspects that I enjoyed in fine arts, but also had very practical elements. It was commercial arts, so you could be artistic, and have a job, and make money.

I also liked a certain structure—the rigor and rules that you had to follow because I think creativity really thrives with limitations. For example, when studying typography you really have to understand the techniques of the font, the kerning and leading and all that stuff.

A good example is my *Word As Image* project. For me, that was when I really started to experiment with typography. I absolutely fell in love with the amazing possibilities you could do with typography. It's worth noting, *Word As Image* really started in my second year in college—in art school. It was one of my first typography assignments. I loved this project because it was so hard to come up with something really good.

[Laughs] Yes, and considering those restrictions you mentioned earlier.

Absolutely! It is restriction because you have to represent the meaning of the word, but only through using typographic elements contained in the letters of that particular word.
In that assignment, you couldn't add anything else. It's almost like a puzzle and you have to follow those rules. But there's an amazing reward when you actually crack that piece of puzzle. I love it.

When I first saw that project I referred to is as the *joy of typography*. It is so evident there really is a lot of joy coming through the work…

Creativity really thrives with limitations.

Exactly! And when I was introduced to the work of Herb Lubalin—his *Word As Images* like *"Families"* or *"Mother and Child,"* in particular—I was amazed at the simplicity and pure conceptual aspects of how, through typography, he was able to show such a clear idea in a visually simple way. So I really enjoyed studying graphic design.

I studied typography, and color theories, and editorial design, and identity design, and packaging design. My school years were really some of the best times. It's also where I began to experiment in new ways, for example a project called *"Universe Revolved: A Three Dimensional Alphabet."* A lot of those typographic projects actually came from my school years.

After I graduated, I was offered a job in a corporate design firm called *Frankfurt Balkind*. They did a lot of annual reports and corporate identities, but the firm doesn't exist anymore. It was really interesting because, at the time of my senior show, I had already accepted the job with them. However, Stefan Sagmeister (Open Manifesto #2) had also came to my senior show and was interested in speaking with me. He was already a well known designer then and said: *"I really love your work and I'd love to talk with you. Why don't you come and visit me in my studio?"* Of course, I went to see him at his studio. It was a small studio in 14th Street—and he offered me a job.

I respectfully declined his job offer because I had already accepted a job. And that's where Stefan became my mentor throughout all these years. He has been an amazing inspiring mentor and that was the beginning of our relationship.

Wow! You turned down the job. Why?

I don't know why. I know I could have gone back to *Frankfurt Balkind* and retracted my acceptance so that I could work with Stefan. But, I didn't. The fact that I had already said yes to the other guys meant I felt I was already committed to them. It was like: *I should honor that commitment*. But, in retrospect, I think it was really the best thing I could have done because I learned so much from working with lots of people in *Frankfurt Balkind*. I think if I had stayed with Stefan, perhaps I would have stayed under his shadow, sort of not being able to flourish on my own. But I guess it's funny; the things that happen when you're in New York, when you're meeting up with all these amazing designers.

After graduating Stefan Sagmesiter offered me a job, but I respectfully declined because I had already accepted a job.

So anyway I went to *Frankfurt Balkind* and some of the best designers I know came out of that firm. Todd St. John was a really amazing designer, and still very much doing amazing work here in New York. He's the principal of *HunterGatherer*.

I also met my best friend Jeff Greenspan there, who is the Chief Creative Officer at *Buzzfeed* now. He has also done some amazing products on his own—personal projects. I met Arturo Ronda there, who I still work with today at *Facebook* and who was also the Creative Director of the Digital Department at *BBDO*.

And they were all originally at *Frankfurt Balkind*?

Yes they were all at *Frankfurt Balkind*. While there I was working mostly on annual reports. I worked on annual reports for *LG*, I worked on annual reports for *NCR (National Company of Registry)*. I worked on identity projects for *Sony*. And although these were not the most exciting creative projects, I learned a lot— how to present the work, how to work in a group, how to be professional. However, by the end of the first year I felt I knew the environment was a bit too corporate and a little too dry and boring for me. And I ended up quitting the job to freelance at Abbott Miller's studio which was called *Design Writing Research*.

He really loved that my portfolio contained lots of conceptual typographic work including *Word As Image* and *Universe Revolved: A Three Dimensional Alphabet*. It so happened that, at the time, he was publishing a book called *Dimensional Typography*, which is kind of a seminal book on 3D typography.

At the time, that was a really interesting book, because it was the first platform to showcase computer generated 3D alphabets and he included the *Universe Revolved*. I did lots of interesting book projects for Abbott while I worked with him. During that time I also worked in other firms like *Tsang Seymour Design*, where I did lots of editorial design and museum catalogs for *Metropolitan Museum of Art (MoMA)*.

I imagine most people would have thought, after leaving *Frankfurt Balkind* you'd be thinking: OK, I've done a year in this firm. I've learned all the rules. It's a bit dry and boring, but it was good discipline. Now, I'll go and knock on Stefan's door,

because he likes my work. But you didn't do that. I know in hindsight it was a good decision but, at the time, what stopped you from immediately going to see Stefan?

I don't really know why I didn't do that. It just never crossed my mind. I always kept in touch with Stefan and showed my projects to him, but for some reason I never really thought about asking to work with him. Actually, I didn't go to Abbott Miller's studio, either. I went to a small firm called *Tsang Seymour Design* first, where I did a bunch of museum catalogs. I have no answer for why I didn't go to Stefan's studio. But, at *Tsang Seymour Design* it was pure editorial work on museum catalogues. It was fun. But, I started to feel the limitations of what the design required; I was really interested in concepts. Designing annual reports and museum catalogs, they weren't necessarily conceptual.

I tried to get as conceptual as possible, but they were mostly aesthetic projects. I grew up in Brazil from the age of 10 to 20, and Brazil is famous for amazing TV and print advertising. I grew up seeing these ads, and I remember being amazed by some of these really funny ads, which became part of the cultural conversation. If there was a famous ad, it would become part of everyday conversations with Brazilians. Advertising creative directors were almost like rock stars.

I really like the fact that conceptual work had huge impact on the society and culture—and on a massive scale. I was interested in the scale and conceptual side of advertising. As a result, I really wanted to find my way into advertising, but I had no connection to the advertising world. So, I kept doing design work.

When I quit *Tsang Seymour Design* I ended up going to Abbott Miller's studio to freelance; while there the 3D *Dimensional Typography* book came out; and, at the same time, there was a *New York Times Sunday Magazine* issue dedicated to innovation in technology. The editor of the *New York Times* saw *Dimensional Typography* and liked my *Universe Revolved* font. She contacted me and asked me if they can use the font for their issue. I said *"Of course!"* They ended up using the font for that issue. It's really funny how one thing leads to another in your life and how the universe has this way of guiding you—opening a door which you least expect.

It's really funny how one thing leads to another in your life, and how the universe has this way of guiding you—opening a door which you least expect.

It's a really interesting example of how these threads—going to Abbott Miller's, being part of *Dimensional Typography*, being part of the *New York Times* magazine—can connect. And at the same time, *Saatchi & Saatchi* was organizing their first *Innovation in Communication* award, which is something Bob Isherwood [former Worldwide Creative Director of *Saatchi & Saatchi*] initiated. They had invited a bunch of famous people, like Buzz Aldrin and Laurie Anderson, who was one of the judges. Laurie saw my font in the *New York Times* magazine, and she loved it. She told the Saatchi people that they should contact me to enter this work to the award, which they did. I was thrilled, and I spent three days preparing this book about the 3D alphabet. I submitted and I became one of the 10 finalists for the innovation award.

That's how I met Bob [Isherwood] for the first time. I remember going to a dinner for the finalists. There's a funny story where I was sitting next to this gentleman who was probably in his 70's. I thought he was one of the Saatchi brothers, because he was in a suit. I even asked if he worked for Saatchi's. Since he didn't I obviously asked what he did do. He said he was an astronaut. I replied: *"Oh, that's incredible. When was the last time you were in space?"* He said *"1969."* It was Buzz Aldrin! That's one of my favorite stories of being in the industry.

And that was my first experience of being exposed to the world of advertising. Bob wanted to see my portfolio, which he loved. He introduced me to the Saatchi people, and I ended up getting hired by *Saatchi & Saatchi*. They doubled my salary and gave me my own office. I thought it was my dream come true. I always wanted to work in advertising, and now I was at one of these famous ad agencies—which I had only heard of when I was growing up. So, I thought: *"Wow, this is it. I'm going to do amazing work and be happy and make a lot of money."*

But when I started working at *Saatchi & Saatchi* I was working projects for *Procter & Gamble, General Mills, Johnson and Johnson*—really huge corporate clients. I realized to produce work was not as easy as I thought.

At the time, it was the height of political correctness in America. Any idea that had any innovative or different angle was getting killed simply because the client did not want to innovate or try new things. They just wanted to do formulaic things, which they knew had worked in the past. Every idea went through testing.

And in the testing stage, every idea got watered down and ended up becoming dull and boring. They always looked for the lowest common denominator. Lawyers were always involved to make sure there was nothing that could be potentially offensive or troublesome. I worked at *Saatchi & Saatchi* for about four years. During those four years I was able to produce one TV spot for *Head and Shoulders* shampoo. One!

I know you left after those four years, but during that time it must have been increasingly disillusioning because of the perception you'd had of *Saatchi & Saatchi*—**because the reputation** *Saatchi & Saatchi* **has; because of the industry you wanted to get into. You were doing more creative work on your own than you were doing being in an 'advertising powerhouse.'**

It was disillusioning. And it was a slow process. I always believed that if I worked hard there would to be opportunities and I would be able to produce work. But ideas got killed. One idea after another—they started getting killed. I began to slowly realize: *"Wow, there's no way that I'm going to be able to produce work here."* Even that one TV spot I mentioned earlier, the one I was able to get out the door. It was for *Head and Shoulders* and was targeting a teenage audience. The TV spot had this guy with his hair on fire, and he was skateboarding down the streets. He jumps into a pool and when he came out it was revealed that the pool was in the shape of *Head and Shoulders*.

It was supposed to be a fun visual spot. The client spent hundreds of thousands of dollars. We shot it in Vancouver. We spent a month shooting it and it was finally aired on TV. The moment it got aired, a few mothers from Texas called the TV station to complain that their kids had told them that they wanted to set their head on fire. It was enough to have one mother to complain for *Procter & Gamble* to cancel that spot. That was it. That was the end of the spot, which we had spent hours and hours, and hundreds of thousands of dollars producing. This is an example of what was happening.

Another experience—which I give in my talks and which is one of my favorite examples—is *Cheerios*. The client was *General Mills* and in the brief they reminded us that *Cheerios* is famous for its classic yellow box. American audiences know the *Cheerios'* yellow box; it has been part of their childhood; it's been an iconic product throughout a generation. In recent years, they had started making other *Cheerios* flavors like 'Honey Nut Cheerios,' 'Multi Grain Cheerios,' and so on. They had five different flavors, all housed in the famous yellow box and they wanted us to communicate that *Cheerios* comes in five different flavors—which is the worst kind of brief. It means they want to show all the products. Our job was to create a billboard to communicate that *Cheerios* comes in five different flavors.

I ended up bringing Jeff Greenspan—my friend from *Frankfurt Balkind* days—to *Saatchi & Saatchi* to work with me as a partner. He's a copywriter. We came up with an idea that showed the five *Cheerios* boxes with the headline: *"Only their holes have the same taste."* When we presented that idea, the client loved it!

When we presented the TV spot, everybody laughed. The clients and agencies were saying: *"This is such a funny idea, we love it."* We were very surprised that a meeting could go so well because we knew how meetings usually went: a really difficult process! But they had such a positive reaction to our idea. We thought: *"Wow, this is amazing."*

As we talked about producing the idea one of the clients raised their hand and said, *"Actually, our corporate term to describe our product is to use flavor instead of taste. We don't really use the word taste to describe our product, we use the term, flavor. How do we turn that into flavor?"*

Our feeling was that: *"Only their holes have the same flavors,"* didn't sound as nice as *"Only their holes have the same taste."* This discussion went on and on for 20 minutes. By the end of the discussion, we were so frustrated about the final outcome—the idea ended up being killed.

That's a classic example of what was happening all the time. The clients or the agency just seeing from their own perspective and not realizing that it doesn't matter. The consumers and the audience don't care if it is the *flavor* or the *taste*. The clients and agencies? They're just talking to themselves.

Those type of experiences just chiseled my excitement away from being in that agency. At the same time, it was very frustrating for me to see the kind of ads that *were* being produced: they were always hitting the lowest common denominator, always boring, and always unimaginative. They weren't even pretty or interesting to look at!

I saw those ads being part of bus stops, subways, and billboards in New York. And it was just a terrible reminder of being part of this agency, this machine, which produced ads that I didn't really appreciate. The worst part was that I was part of this machine.

Which is very different to Brazil.

Exactly. Right! Yes. In Brazil, I remember seeing amazing ads that took risks, potentially offended people, and were funny. Brazil is not politically correct. People have a great sense of humor. You can talk about sex in a way that's not offensive. America is a very prudish country, so we can't talk about sex, or race—you can't talk about anything. In the end, you end up having this really watered down boring stuff.

It's interesting when we look at it from different cultural perspectives. If we consider America and Europe—actually, lets just take America because you're pretty disillusioned and critical of the traditional advertising agency model there— what do you think the future of the advertising agency looks like?

Thankfully, I think they're now being forced to adopt a whole new mechanism if they want to be relevant because of what is referred to as "Social marketing" via *Facebook*, *Twitter*, and *Instagram*. The traditional method of one-way broadcast doesn't work any more. The content agencies are creating has to be *retweeted, liked, shared,* and *pinned*. This gives consumers the power to make the message heard, to be shared and broadcasted on the agency's (or client's) behalf. Traditionally, you were basically forced to look at an ad, to watch it in between a TV program. Traditionally, you were forced to look at the ads in a magazine. Nowadays, a lot of people are spending time on their social media. The way it works with social media is people have to share and spread the message on the brand's behalf. There's a fundamental shift in the way these messages are created and shared.

A lot of the agencies are adapting and some of the agencies are more successful than others. But it's a completely different way of presenting content. It has to be real time. You don't have as much time as before, where you could have months of planning for your TV spot. Now, brands like *Oreo* are reacting in real time. For example, when there was a *Superbowl* blackout, they were publishing on their page about the blackout because they want to be part of the conversation with people—in real time. That's why a media platform like *Buzzfeed* is so successful. Now, brands have to be part of that conversation.

If we go back to your original desire to get into the creative field, you were interested in art. Then you went into design, and then advertising, and so on. Initially, I guess there was an *art versus design* question for you, so do you see your personal projects as art or design? For example, the [American] *ABC News* report covering *The Bubble Project* described you as an "artist." Then, there's your *Delete Billboard* project, which could be classified as "street art." And, of course, your *miniature models* have been exhibited at *MAD [Museum of Art and Design]*. Considering your personal work, do you see them as art, as design, as ideas? How would you describe them?

I talked to Stefan about this and asked him this specific question: *"Do you see yourself as an artist or a designer?"* He's adamant about calling himself a "designer." He doesn't believe he is an artist. I disagree, I think he is an artist. I consider myself as an artist, too, but I use the technique of design, street art, and simulation through the different kinds of media. I think I'm all of it: I'm a designer, an artist, a street artist, an instillation artist, a web designer—a little bit of lots of things.

This new breed of creative we're seeing in advertising and design have a tendency to be multifaceted. When I used to work at *Google Creative Lab* we hired people who were multifaceted. They had to know how to work in video format, be a great designer, be able to create their own content, and they should be able to code—because that's how we communicate nowadays. You're not only doing TV spots if you work in advertising, you also have to also come with an idea for a website; you have to come up with an idea for *Facebook* page posts; you have to be able to create an app, or a game. It's all of that. And it's a good thing.

When we consider your experience in the advertising world, particularly the politically correct advertising world of America, your personal work is the extreme opposite. One could argue it's even subversive—humorously so. Even right through to your *"White Feed"* project, it's humorously subversive in a nice way. Is that a direct response to some of the experiences you've had, or is it simply a personal approach?

Perhaps, yes. '*Subversion*' is a word I hear a lot from other people when they're describing my work. Again, I never purposely tell myself: "*I want something subversive.*" I think there's a part of me that always enjoyed being a little bad boy.

[Laughs]

I don't know where that's coming from, but I like to be provocative and I like to be subversive. Some of it is a reaction to my experience of being in a corporate world, my frustrations of not being able to create great work that I believe could benefit the brand, the consumer, and the agency. So yes, I think part of it is a response to what I've experienced. And I love using humor as a method of disguising, or softening a subversive message because once people smile and laugh, their guard is down, which means they're more susceptible to new ideas.

As a matter of interest, because *The Bubble Project* **was quite subversive—and described by many as being illegal—have the authorities knocked on your door, considering your identity is now pretty well established?**

Yes, I plastered over 30,000 stickers and I continue to do so. Not in the massive scale that I used to—back in the day. Over the (many) years I've been *bubbling*, I got caught by police on the streets and in subways. They stopped me and gave me violation tickets directly.

Were you in disguise?

I never walk around disguised because that would be counterproductive and would draw more attention to me. I'm only in disguise when I'm giving interviews. If I walked around like that everybody is going to look at me.

[Laughs] Of course!

You don't want people saying: "*Who's that weird guy?*" The disguise is just for interviews, but it's also about being theatrical because anybody is able to find out who's behind this project. The most threatening thing that I experienced through *The Bubble Project* was the very serious letter from a lawyer representing the media agency, *Clear Channel*. They own lots of the billboards and bus stop space where they advertise. The lawyer's letter was pretty threatening and called for me to stop *bubbling* or they'd take legal action.

I was scared, and I didn't know what to do so I hired a lawyer. In a way, this goes back to your original question about making projects participatory. One of the many benefits is you're not the sole person who's responsible for this project. A lot of people were *bubbling*. They took the template, cut it out and pasted it on their own, or made their own bubble spheres.

In the end, I wrote to the *Clear Channel* lawyers and said I had personally stopped *bubbling*, but there are other people who are still *bubbling* and I have no control over that. I never heard from them again.

That makes sense. Even when you yourself were *bubbling*, you're also collaborating with the public. You'd paste a sticker and then the public would essentially graffiti on that sticker. I guess if they were going to sue Ji Lee they'd have to also sue everyone that wrote on a Ji Lee bubble sticker—and that would be impossible.

I think they were mostly concerned about the act of putting the stickers on top of an ad. The fact that some of them were removable stickers—when you rip it, some of the sticker stays, but it's not spray painted graffiti you might see on a wall, which is harder to remove. That is seen as a more serious crime.

I imagine you didn't approach *The Bubble Project* with any of this in mind. I assume it was fortuitous that stickers was the medium you were using.

Yeah. I'm very thankful that I went through this very frustrating experience of dealing with the corporation. If things had gone more or less well in the [*Saatchi & Saatchi*] agency, I don't think I'd ever be focusing on my personal projects. One of the things I like to focus on in my talks is that frustrations are the best motivation, the best inspiration to do meaningful work.

Another project I was working on at the time at *Saatchi & Saatchi* was for *General Mills*. They wanted to come up with some kind of social awareness campaign to fight child obesity, and I was briefed to open this project. I came up with this idea: what if parents and their kids could communicate about the issue in a different way? For example, we would make magnetized bubble stickers they could use on the refrigerator.

They could then each write fun messages to one another about food, for example: *"Hey, Billy don't forget to eat your vegetables today"*. We would use this fun graphic device—which kids are familiar with in comic strips—as a platform for parents and children to communicate to each other about healthy eating.

Then, of course, that idea got killed, too, because... I don't know why, or whatever the corporate reasons were. I had really thought there was no way they'd kill this idea because it was for a social, positive awareness program. But they killed it! It was at this point I realized: I can't depend on the client, I can't depend on the agency to produce any good ideas. So I have to do everything myself. I'm just going to take on this project and do it on my own!

I decided to make the bubble stickers and, somehow, made the connection of putting those stickers on the ads in the street—the ones I hated so much. I spent around $3,000, produced 30,000 stickers and started to put them on ads in the streets.

At the time, it was a really therapeutic thing for me because for every ad that got killed, I didn't mind anymore. I could just go out and create hundreds of new ads because *bubbling* transformed the boring ads into really fascinating things. Those speech bubble stickers completely changed the way people saw those ads. It became a real therapy for me.

Going back to the original question, that's when I realized the power of opening up to participation with others because a lot of people started writing amazing things inside the bubbles. After a few months, it blew up and it's all because of the Internet. Without the Internet, I think *The Bubble Project* would've been a quarter of the project it became.

This was also the first time I truly realized the power of the Internet because, in the beginning, I set up the website and I posted, maybe, hundreds of pictures. From this I was getting 30 to 50 visitors a day. But one day, I went to check the number of visitors and it had gone up to 50,000 visitors!

It was at this point I realized: I can't depend on the client, I can't depend on the agency to produce any good ideas. So I have to do everything myself. I'm just going to take on this project and do it on my own!

Did you promote it in any way, or did that shift in response just sort of happen by itself?

I didn't promote it at all. I shared it with my friends, but that's about it. I actually thought the increased number was some kind of mistake. But the next time I checked the website it had crashed because there were so many people visiting it!

And I realized it had happened because *boingboing.net*—which at the time was the biggest blog—had featured a small, tiny story about *The Bubble Project*. Because of that one little post, it really (and completely) changed my life. Tons of people started coming to the website: newspapers, and TVs and everybody wanted to make a story about it. I had no idea this was going to be such a big deal. But from the response I realized I can create a project—on my own—which can touch millions of people around the world. I can do everything myself. I can come up with an idea. I can finance the idea. I can market this idea. And I can put together a website.

The thing is, at the time I didn't know how to design a website so I went to *Barnes and Noble* and bought a book on *Dreamweaver*. I read it and, step by step, built this website.

It was such an empowering and liberating experience for me. My perception before was that, in order to produce an idea and get it out there, I needed a client, I needed money, I needed an agency, I needed the publishers. *The Bubble Project* was such an eye-opening experience because it proved I can do everything myself—with the help of the Internet.

That would pretty much be the antithesis of your experience at a big agency like *Saatchi & Saatchi* where, as you said, you'd spent months doing an ad, with a budget of hundreds of thousands of dollars, with lawyers involved, with numerous people you needed to keep happy, as well as needing to secure media placements. Essentially, with the *The Bubble Project* you simply used one of the foundation stones of advertising—the power of an idea...

Exactly...

And then just put that idea into the world, but in an incredibly economical, efficient way. And in a participatory way, as well.

Yeah, and I think more and more people are realizing the possibilities of this. It's wonderful to see so many amazing projects. Are you familiar with the project *"Humans of New York"*?

It's a *Tumblr* blog and also a *Facebook* page developed by a New York photographer who put together the project. He simply goes around taking pictures of interesting people in New York, and talks about their story. It really blew up. I think he has hundreds of thousands of followers, and he was interviewed in all kinds of TV stations. Again, it's just one person going around, taking pictures, and just showing interesting stories about New Yorkers. Anyone can do that. You don't need a publisher. You don't need an agency or a client behind it to fund the project and make it famous. Any individual today can make that happen.

If we go back to your earlier point about how conservative corporate clients are in America and the experience you had at *Saatchi & Saatchi*, **this is in stark contrast to the small risk you took to do** *The Bubble Project.* **Yet, you received immense participation from the public. And within a relatively short space of time you received significant media coverage, which those agency clients would kill or die to get—but they're simply not brave enough to take what I refer to as a 'considered risk,' which is pretty much what you've done...**

Yeah, because they live in fear. They are afraid to experiment with anything new because of the potential negative consequences. This is such a negative mindset—a very fearful mindset—and is the exact opposite of the mindset expected of a creative agency or an innovative brand. The ironic thing is that, because of *The Bubble Project,* a lot of agencies wanted to hire me to work as a freelancer or full time. And these were agencies who were making the ads that I was defacing in the streets!

My stance on *The Bubble Project* has always been that I was not destroying their ads. Through *The Bubble Project,* I truly believe I was helping those brands, simply because people were now actually looking at their ads. Otherwise they would have been ignored, but now people are participating and commenting on the ads that they see. I felt it was a win-win for everyone. For the brands: because they were getting more eyes looking at their ads; for the consumer: who had the opportunity to talk back to the advertisement (and the brand); and for me: who is having a lot of fun doing all these things on the side.

This is another extremely important thing for me: the idea of having fun. I think a lot of us who are in the creative field, we're doing this because we have such a passion and get so much fun doing what we do. We didn't go to law school, we didn't go to business school, to make money. We went into the creative business because we feel we have passion and we love doing what we do.

It's all about having fun. That was the reason for me joining the advertising industry. From the outside, it seemed to be such a fun job. You're traveling around, going to places, coming up with ideas—and these ideas get produced, and lot of people love it. It just seemed like a lot of fun to be doing this. But the reality was very different: it really wasn't fun. In fact, it was the opposite of fun.

If we look at *The Bubble Project*, and how you just described the win-win scenario for everybody involved, and helping those brands. There's something that I find really interesting, and which I've heard you speak about before: it's the idea of *hacking*. We generally associate negative things with the term hacking, but if we take *The Bubble Project* it's a constructive, humorous, participatory hacking of an advert, which ultimately provides the brand with information they could never really find if they hired a marketing company tasked with uncovering honest feedback. The idea of hacking, in a positive way, to something that is already there, is this a central part of what you enjoy?

Yeah, I think hacking or hijacking is a reoccurring technique in the work that I do. I also feel at home right now working with *Facebook* because the entire culture of *Facebook* is also based on hack. In the world of *Facebook* the word *Hack* is plastered everywhere because Mark Zuckerberg is a hacker himself. It's our mission to really change the perception of what 'hack' is because, for the most part, when people think about hackers they think about those people who steal your bank account, identity, money, and spam you—stuff like that. But hacking, or hijacking, is really the simplest way of taking what already exists and turning it into something new, making it your own, but in a very simple, ingenious, creative way.

Hacking, or hijacking, is really the simplest way of taking what already exists and turning it into something new, making it your own, but in a very simple, ingenious, creative way.

Like when you copy a line of code, and change a couple of things, then paste them to make it your own code. You save a lot of energy, and time, and resources than if you had to create your line of code from scratch. It's an extremely efficient way and people either use that for good or bad. If you think about the terrorists of 9/11, they didn't have the bomb because to produce the bomb would take a lot of time, and technology, and energy, and money. So they hijacked an airplane and used that as a bomb, which is an extremely efficient way for terrorists to achieve their objective. Of course, it is terrible, but it is an example.

But also, from a creative standpoint, you can take what already exists. In my case I took advertisements in New York City, and then I just used this little sticker device which completely changed the meaning of these ads.

If you look at a lot of the editorial art I do for *New York Times*, for example I did a cover for *Time Magazine* which depicts the *Statue of Liberty* holding surveillance cameras. The concept was in response to the Boston bombing: we have to give up our freedom for protection, for security. Other examples are where I created the dead *Wall Street bull* and the *fat Christ*. A lot of the stuff you see in my editorial art has to do with hacking.

I take really well known, iconic images—those which are universally well known—and I just change something, which completely changes the meaning. That's so much more efficient than if I created a whole new message and try to communicate that idea from scratch.

Perhaps this echoes what the legendary Bob Gill (Open Manifesto #3) passionately believes: in order to do work that is meaningful and has impact, you need to have something interesting to say first.

Absolutely!

This seems to be a recurring theme with you, too—from the *Time Magazine* cover you just described right back to *The Bubble Project*. They are fun. They are participatory. They are driven by self-interest, but in an enlightened way because others benefit from the work. They are humorous. They're a bit subversive. They're based in an idea. But, above all, you've got something

to say. That's probably the most critical point to highlight for anybody who wants to go out and make an impact.

Yes, you're absolutely right. I think what you are referring to is *content*. The message and concept. In fact they are very similar things. *The Bubble Project* was borne from my frustration of seeing ads and I wanted to say something about it. I wanted to highlight the fact that the ads were bullshit. We never asked for ads to be in public spaces. Why is it we're forced to look at these horrible ads? I wanted to have a discussion around that. That was my message.

It's great when I'm doing editorial art for the *New York Times* or *Time Magazine*, because they already come with a strong message. They have a point of view. I use this as a vehicle to communicate a message. Sometimes I inject my own personal view on the subject.

But I'm only interested in doing something that has an idea. Even if you look at the *Parallel World* project, which is an upside down miniature world. For some, this might seem like a delightful piece of art. But for me, it also has a message. For me the interesting point is that we, sort of, live in the *The Matrix*. I don't think we're very different from what is portrayed in that movie, where we're just programs made by a machine and we're just living our lives mindlessly and meaninglessly to produce energy for the machines.

Although we're not products of machines, I believe that perhaps most of us are products of societies. We're products of our parents. We're a product of our educational institutions, where we're told to live in a certain way, and we don't really question those things. I mean, why does the alphabet have to be two dimensional? Why does it have to be read from left to right, top to bottom? Who set those rules? Why don't we ever question these fundamental things? Why does art have to be always hung on the wall? Why don't we ever hang stuff on the ceiling?

We live in this matrix of rules and conventions, which we are told about at a very early age. So much so, that we simply don't question them. For me, my side projects are an exercise in breaking those conventions. In the case of the *Parallel World* project, the hope is that people might look at the ceiling with

I wanted to highlight the fact that the ads were bullshit. We never asked for ads to be in public spaces. Why is it we're forced to look at these horrible ads? I wanted to have a discussion around that. That was my message.

completely different eyes. Maybe this will prompt people to look at the alphabet and realize: *"Hey, I don't always have to read from left to right. I can read stuff from right to left and letters can be unconventional. Letters can also be set in motion. They can be stacked from bottom up."*

I'm always interested in this idea of breaking out and—through humor and through delight—encouraging people to realize we don't have to look at the world with a conventional kind of viewpoint.

Taking your point, and in terms of typography, there is a wonderful quote from Zuzana Licko of *Emigre* where, in the 90s, she commented on the legibility wars: *"We read best what we read most."* **It comes down to conventions and the mainstream. Whatever we read most is what we are familiar with and anything else is usually not accepted. Whereas Licko is simply saying we can challenge things, because the more we challenge them, the more mainstream they become—and the more acceptable they become. In terms of new thinking, I guess the message is: Get it out there; Challenge things; Help it become mainstream. In some ways, this kind of sums up what you've just been saying.**

Yeah, absolutely. I agree with that. There is a fascinating project by the really famous violin player, Joshua Bell. He's world famous and he played his Bach sonatas in a Washington DC subway for an hour. Literally, nobody stopped to listen. The following day played at *Carnegie Hall*, and people paid $200 to come and listen to him—using the same violin and playing the same music. That just shows that we're not awake. We don't really pay attention to what's around us, because we are just so trapped in our own matrix.

So I like to create projects like *The Bubble Project* and *Parallel World* as a means to create a little crack in the matrix, as a means to stop a person—even if it is for two seconds—to stop them and to be in the moment, to get them out of the mindless zone.

As a matter of interest, we've been talking about your projects and your experience in advertising, etc. But what was the transition like from *Droga5* to *Google Creative Lab* and then to *Facebook*, where you are now Creative Lead? It must be a very different experience to that of an advertising agency.

When I joined *Droga5* it was, for me, the epitome of the creative scene. I really had an amazing time working with David [Droga]. I think I was something like 'employee number seven' at the time.

Really? [laughs]

He had just opened the *Droga5* agency. It was essentially a startup. Things were chaotic and fun. I worked on some of my best advertising projects, including the *New Museum*.

I really had a great time. There was certainly no corporate fear. David is a fearless leader and we believed in our ideas and would not take on a client who didn't understand the creativity. It was really as good as an agency can be.

The irony is that David comes from the *Saatchi & Saatchi* stable...

Exactly.

It's almost the antithesis—with *Saatchi & Saatchi* being the finishing school for both of you, if you like, to then set up *Droga5* and be the absolute opposite of what *Saatchi & Saatchi* was doing at the time.

Yeah. Well, he was more fortunate in creating amazing work because for several years he was in *Saatchi & Saatchi* offices in Asia where things are a little less rigid, and there are opportunities to do great work. He was producing all the best work for *Saatchi & Saatchi* while he was in Asia. I think he also felt limited by corporate policies and he wanted to do things his own way. I was very fortunate to be able to be part of his response to that. He hired me on the spot when he saw *The Bubble Project*. It wasn't because of my advertising work, because I really had no advertising work in my portfolio. Again, another benefit of doing personal projects!

So I worked at *Droga5*, but there were a couple of things that I was never able to connect with in the agency world. First, the whole emphasis on winning awards. That's very strongly present everywhere, including *Droga5*. I never really cared about winning awards. For me, it was more important to do work that really helped a client sell his or her products. That's my job. But to do so in a way that is creative, in way that's motivating, in a way that's engaging to the consumer.

I thought things like creating puns or creating jingles were extremely effective and you can do it in a way that's also creative. These things aren't highly regarded in the award's world. There are certain formulas people use to win awards. I never really understood people's interest in creating work to win awards.

Also, I had a very tough time working for a brand that I didn't really believe in. For example, certain sodas [soft drinks], which I didn't drink but had to spend hours and months trying to crack a creative solution for. I had to do it, because that's my job. But I had a hard time really pouring my heart into it because I either didn't enjoy the product or I didn't believe in that brand.

I think, I was getting a little disillusioned about what it meant to be working in advertising industry in general. At that stage I'd been doing that for almost 10 years. Then I got a call from *Google*. It was Robert Wong, who I actually met at *Frankfurt Balkind* when we both worked there.

It's sounds like *Frankfurt Balkind* was an amazing company: the best kind of finishing school! [laughs]

I know. Working there was actually an amazing blessing in disguise. In retrospect, it was actually a great decision not to join Stefan's studio.

So Robert Wong called because he had just joined *Google* and he had just started *Google Creative Lab*. He asked if I wanted to join him. For me, it was a no-brainer because I believed in *Google*, and I used their product—and it was free. The mission of the company is to make information free and accessible to everyone. Here was a company that I really believed in. So I joined *Google* in a heartbeat. Again, I was really fortunate to be one of the first employees at *Google Creative Lab*. It was an amazing experience. I worked there for three years with some of the most talented and brightest people I'd ever worked with before.

One thing about working at *Google Creative Lab,* which was really liberating and wonderful and which was very different to working at an agency, was that everybody was working together towards the same goal, regardless of whether you were from the account side, if you were an engineer, if you were the manager, they were all amazing and talented—and they were all working together towards the same goal.

Whereas, in an ad agency there is a huge split between the creative department and the accounting department. There's antagonisms and often a lot of friction. There's a mistrust. The two sides don't really like each other. Creative people usually despise account people and account people think creative people are spoiled divas.

Not having that kind of division was, for me, an amazing experience. And just in general, to work for a brand that did amazing things for the world and which I truly believed in from my heart, made my world easy. It was just a pleasure for me to go to work every day.

It was a big transition for me, and a blessing to be part of that experience. I learned a lot about technology and the impact of technology, to really understand about how to be 'scrappy' because, at the beginning of *Google Creative Lab,* we didn't have the same kind of resources that ad agencies have.

For example, when we did the *Chrome* campaign, I went to *Times Square* with an intern to interview people. We asked one question: *What is a browser?* That resulting video got almost 800,000 views. I would never have thought to do this if I were in the creative agency side because there is a producer, there is a film maker that you hire, a videographer and you hire an editor...

But because *Google Creative Lab* was new there was no such thing as a creative department. We had to do things on our own. We had to go out there, take our video cameras, find an editor or we edited it ourselves with *iMovie* and just learn everything, right down to how to upload to *YouTube.*

For me, that was an amazing and enlightening experience; allowing me to understand that the best way to do things is to do it on your own. And by doing this thing on your own, you're learning the most.

It reminds me of something I read about *Facebook*, **which stated all of the executives, including Mark Zuckerberg, aren't seen as executives, they're seen as 'entrepreneurial thinkers' who actually get involved with the work, who get their hands dirty at ground level—they're not removed from the process. It sounds similar to what you just described with** *Google Creative Lab*, **where you weren't removed from the**

process of producing the actual work. It seems there's a correlation between the philosophy of *Facebook* and the philosophy of *Google Creative Lab*. Everyone gets in, everyone gets involved regardless of your position in the company. Would that be true?

Absolutely true. Which is also very different to the advertising world, where there are ranks and hierarchies. The creative directors are mostly approving the ideas. They're not really getting their hands dirty. Oftentimes, they're not even coming up with ideas themselves because they're so busy managing the accounts. They have teams of art directors and copywriters who are coming up with the ideas. Whereas, at a place like *Google Creative Lab*, at the time I was there, and now at *Facebook*—especially *Facebook*—it's a very flat organization. Physically, if you visit the office there are no separate rooms. Everybody's sitting on one giant floor. Mark Zuckerberg is sitting amongst engineers and product designers. And Sheryl Sandberg will be sitting there, too. It's really a culture of entrepreneurs.

As a manager, you have to ship stuff. There is a huge emphasis on people shipping things. You see this word 'ship' appear in lots of internal communications—in posters, in emails, etc. In fact, your performance is only measured by what you ship. I really fit right in because I love to make stuff, I love to ship. If I don't, I get nervous.

That's part of the reason why I was having such a hard time at *Saatchi & Saatchi* in the beginning. It's very seductive, because you have a high salary, you have a great office, a very supporting...

And a prestigious business card.

And a prestigious business card! You can get easily sucked into that... comfortable life. When you have kids and mortgage to pay, it's very hard to leave that kind of seduction and security. But, at *Facebook,* it's a completely different way of working. You really have to get your hands dirty and ship stuff. I like it. I feel most liberated, useful, and alive when I'm making things and shipping stuff.

Let's talk about the entrepreneurial attitude of *Facebook*, and considering the trajectory of your career. A lot of your

side projects have been hugely successful and internationally recognized. They've led you to other jobs—jobs you feel you'd never have had otherwise. Yet, you continue to work for other companies, rather than creating your own studio or agency, which would turn your side projects into a business. Is there a particular reason for the decision not to do this?

I've thought about doing that. Maybe starting my own design firm, doing my own thing, having my own startup. Those thoughts have always been present. But the experience of working at *Google Creative Lab* and the experience of working with *Facebook* has been so rewarding. Also, I learned so much by being part of these organizations. I work with some of the brightest people, whom I learn from every day. It's all fine as long as I can maintain the balance between my personal projects and professional projects. I'm a big believer that these two worlds complement each other.

Things that I learn doing side projects—meaning I'm doing things on my own and making things—I can bring these experiences into what I do with *Facebook*, because now I know how to make stuff and ship stuff, which is valued by the company. Things that I learn at *Google Creative Lab* and *Facebook*—with regards the power of technology and the latest tools on how to amplify your message, how media works, how to collaborate with people from different disciplines—I bring this to my personal projects, which end up becoming these amazing self-fueling systems. I see the benefit of being part of these two worlds.

Fortunately, both *Google Creative Lab* and *Facebook* have no issues with me doing side projects or personal projects. They even encourage it. I got hired by these two companies because of my personal projects. So, obviously, they see the value in that. They see the value in their employees being entrepreneurs.

I don't have to be at work at a certain time. There is trust that I'm doing my work. As long as I'm delivering and shipping, they're cool. This gives me more flexibility and freedom to do things that I need to do. It really works well. For now, I'm pretty happy.

Perhaps you don't see it this way, but considering your personal projects—which have attracted companies like *Droga5* and *Google Creative Lab* and *Facebook*—these side projects and

personal projects have helped you develop your own personal brand. Is that something that you've intentionally tried to do or is it a by-product? Would you even encourage other people to look at their side projects or personal projects as a means to perhaps create a personal brand?

It's definitely a by-product. It's not something that I've intentionally tried to do when I started doing these personal projects. As I did personal projects I realized: *"Wow, I'm getting calls from agencies. I'm getting calls from great companies to join them to work with them."* When I started doing *The Bubble Project*, I didn't even think about naming it as personal projects. I just did it because I needed to do it and I wanted to do it. The more projects I did the more I realized there's a benefit—not only a personal benefit, but also a professional benefit.

After a while I realized I can actually focus on—as you said— branding this as my personal branding tool, for my personal activities. I go around the world giving speeches and presenting at conferences, which I love to do, and I also work for companies that I love and believe in. That's why I make a clear distinction on my website between personal projects and professional projects, which is a way of helping me position myself to the market because the personal things I do also help professionally.

I see a lot of examples where people are doing this. People like Jeff Greenspan, my partner at *Saatchi & Saatchi* together with Ivan Cash. Justin Gedak, Christoph Niemann; these are people who really have branded themselves doing lots of personal projects. And they're also extremely successful professionally.

There may be a simple reason why they are successful. If you put talent aside—and even if you put profile aside—something you talk about quite a lot is that you can be more successful in a project when you've got total control over it. This is where the side projects allow you to create a personal brand, which is specific to how you want to be portrayed. It's having that control.

You're absolutely right. It's very hard, as you know, doing a professional project where you can't have that level of control, because there's so many chefs in the kitchen. There's a client. There's a creative director. There's a lawyer. There's an account manager. They all have their opinions, and they're not less important than your opinion. But, as soon as you involve so many people who want to control the project, it becomes something completely different from what you envisioned. Yes, you're right. When I'm doing my personal projects I have complete control to do things exactly the way I want to do things, so that's hugely important.

Just a couple of final questions. On a more serious note, the wider role of social media is increasing. We've seen this with the *Arab Spring*. We've seen this with the horrendous Boston bombings where social media, particularly *Twitter* and *Reddit*, shaped the news channels' narrative, because it focused on immediate reports from people who were on the scene. Of course, this is good in some ways but it's a hindrance in other ways. For example, the *FBI* had to respond to people who were incorrectly identifying the bombers. Although those accusations were incorrect, the *FBI* still had to investigate because people on the ground were tweeting or posting.

With this in mind, does this increasing influence of social media in any way influence how you would approach your position at *Facebook*, even at a creative leadership level?

That's a complex question. Anything that's powerful has both good and bad; has both the potential to be great and awful. That touches on what we talked about earlier, the power of hijacking or hacking, right?

Now the Internet is accessible and available for anybody, you can use that tool to do something great like start a revolution. But, you can also use it to steal people's identity and go into their bank account. It's the nature of anything that becomes powerful. I believe in the goodness of people. I'm a positive person. I am an optimistic person. I prefer to see—and tend to see—the positive before I see the negative. When I work on a project on behalf of *Facebook*, or on my personal projects, I never really see the negative things. My mindset is positive; my mindset is that this is going to turn into a positive project.

Obviously, you cannot be naive and ignore important things to protect people's privacy and stuff like that, but there's something about that mindset that attracts positive energy around it.

When I'm doing my personal projects I have complete control to do things exactly the way I want to do things, so that's hugely important.

The best thing I can do is to be informed about the tools and technologies that could potentially be used for negative purposes. That's what I do: I try to be as informed as possible about things that happen in the news.

In terms of the power of social media platforms—even the very name we give them, 'social media'—they're moving out of the social side and moving into influencing the news media cycle. Could you ever see Mark Zuckerberg say: *"Social media is growing up, into another form of media, which is not necessarily social."* **Although social media is participatory, is it possible that** *Facebook* **might become more of a media power player rather than just a platform for people to participate?**

Facebook's stance is that it is a medium—and it is a media platform. Our goal is to be the most effective, fastest, and most efficient tool for people to build on top of this platform. That's why we want to stay as neutral as possible when it comes to having an opinion on content. Our goal is to build the best product possible. It's really up to people to decide whatever they want to do with this powerful medium and powerful tool. You can also see this with *Google* and others, like *Reddit*. You know the theory of singularity? It's where the technology is evolving at such a rapid speed that we actually don't know what's going to happen.

One can say the same about where social media is going. In fact, we really don't know where this is going, because it's so fast. It's evolving so quickly. As someone who works at *Facebook*, I can feel things are constantly changing within the company. In a way, it's the most unstable workplace, because the product is constantly changing. People are moving from one group to another.

But it's also extremely liberating, because it's not rigid and resistant to change compared to places like the corporate creative agencies that I used to work in. That's all about stability and status quo. Now, I work in the exact opposite environment to that—an environment that is all about change, speed, innovation, and constant iterations in real time.

There are two sides. It can be extremely liberating and extremely innovative and creative, but, at the same time, there is acute uncertainty, an instability that comes from working in an environment like this.

Which I imagine is both exciting and scary.

Yeah. It's both exciting and unsettling at the same time.

I'm going to finish by hacking my own question. I was originally going to focus on two of your philosophies which I really love: *"Ideas are nothing, doing is everything"* **and** *"Ship, ship, ship"*, **because inherent in these is a belief that one must have the courage to produce things, rather than just simply conceptualize them. However, instead I'd like to go back to your very first firm—***Frankfurt Balkind***—where many of the people that you now work with or associate with came from. Obviously, as we discussed earlier, there's a tangible benefit in creating your own personal brand. In the same way, there is a tangible benefit in fostering a really valued and collaborative network of people, which in your case goes right back to the beginning of your career. Is this something that you continue to consciously foster, having had the benefit of that initial group of people? Or, is it something that's just simply organic and natural?**

I'm increasingly more aware of the importance of 'the network' and connections with people. In fact, my job at *Facebook* is really to help. I have two roles: the first is to help some of the biggest brands in the world with marketing on *Facebook*. In doing so, I work with the brands directly as well as their creative agencies to publish and create apps, because they all need help in these areas. The other side of my role is to communicate the constantly changing, evolving—and sometimes confusing—tools and messages about *Facebook* to creative agencies, in order to show the amazing potential these creative agencies will have through understanding and working with the *Facebook* platform.

You mentioned earlier that creative agencies often talk about, or think about *Facebook*, in terms of putting it in the *social media bucket,* alongside *Twitter, Pinterest, Buzzfeed,* and so on. However, I believe *Facebook* is the defining medium of our time. Over one billion people are tuned into it, and over 700 million people in the United States alone are logging in every day, spending hours on *Facebook*. Yet, still, the vast majority of creative agencies are just scratching the surface, in terms of the potential of using *Facebook* as a platform.

I work closely with agencies. I'm constantly in contact with Creative Directors, Art Directors and Executive Creative Directors of agencies—just engaging with them and really sharing what can be done, discussing the potential. These connections are really important. And it's extremely important to be humble. It's vital to really listen to what they're looking for and what they're confused about, what their point of view is, and why they may not be considering *Facebook*. A lot of this is just connecting with them and having a general interest in what they're doing—and then humbly sharing my view of what can be done with this platform. It all goes back to the original point of having meaningful connections with people.

Throughout my career, there were times that I was arrogant and cocky, simply because I felt frustrated. In some cases, I didn't really respect the kind of work the agency was doing. Now, I'm realizing that kind of arrogance and cockiness is only self destructive. It doesn't really create anything positive or meaningful, or constructive. These days I spend a lot of time and energy even writing an email—being a little more caring. I try to put myself in the receiver's position and try to be as warm and personal as possible.

I'm so busy. I'm constantly juggling stuff. It's easier to hit that reply button as soon as possible. But because I see the value of a personal connection with everybody, I really try to put extra effort in connecting with people in a more meaningful way. In the end, that's the most important asset: friendships and the connections with people.

Give and Take

Kevin Finn in conversation with Adam Grant

Kevin Finn: Can you briefly describe the difference between a *giver*, a *taker* and a *matcher*?

Adam Grant: I think of these as three different styles of interaction. The *takers* are people who love to get as much as possible from others and never want to give anything back, unless they absolutely have to. That usually means they're trying to hog all of the interesting and visible projects and leave the grunt work for everybody else they collaborate with—and yet walk away with the majority of the credit when the work is done.

At the other end of the spectrum, we have people that I call *givers*. I don't necessarily mean a philanthropist or a volunteer, but rather the kind of person who enjoys helping others—and frequently does it without any strings attached. *Givers* are often sharing their knowledge, making introductions, maybe providing mentoring or just stepping up to help their colleagues.

Then, in the middle of that spectrum, we have *matchers*, who are people that like to keep an even balance of 'give and take.' It's quid pro quo. If I'm a *matcher*, and I was to do you a favor, I would expect an equal one back. And if you were to do me a favor, I might feel like I was in debt until I settled the score.

There seems to be an insatiable market for advice on 'how to be successful,' and this advice ranges from being shallow through to being insightful. However, in your book *Give and Take* **you quote Keith Ferrazzi who employs a deceptively simple rule.** *"I'll sum up the key to success in one word—generosity."* **Now, that goes to your definition of a** *giver*, **but is that too simplistic? A key to success being** *generosity*?

Well, I think it's half of the story, for sure. I think the key to success is also the key to failure.

Very true... [Laughing]

As we know, one of the things that I found most fascinating with doing the research for *Give and Take*, is when you compare *givers*, *takers*, and *matchers*. Across engineering, and medicine, and sales, you find that the *givers* are typically the worst performers, so they tend to have the lowest productivity in engineering, the worst grades in medical school and the lowest sales revenue.

They are also the best performers. [Laughs] It's the *givers* who are at the very top of those metrics: the highest engineering productivity, the best medical grades, and even the highest sales revenue. *Takers* and *matchers* are more likely to have average performance.

I think Keith really captures part of that puzzle in highlighting how part of that generosity can accelerate your career. But if you're not careful, it can also sink your career.

I guess the big question for a lot of people would be: how can you remain a *giver*, and avoid being—what you describe as—a 'doormat'? You've just highlighted a really good case in point where the same fields of industry or professional practice have a hugely successful *and* hugely unsuccessful *giver*. How can one manage that?

Well, I think a lot of it has to do with recognizing that successful *givers* aren't necessarily altruistic. They're not so selfless that they put other people's interests ahead of their own all the time. Rather, what they try to do is integrate their desire to help others with their own goals and ambitions. To your question about the 'doormat effect,' I think that can play out in a couple of different ways.

One of [laughs] the great ways to get exploited is to give relentlessly to *takers*. What I find is that successful *givers* are much more likely to say, *"Look, if you're going to be a 'taker,' then I'm going to shift my style and become a 'matcher'—only give to you if you're willing to reciprocate by paying it back, or paying it forward."*

Instead, they are likely to give most generously to *givers*, who do tend to 'pay it forward,' and *matchers*, who tend to pay it back. I think the rest of the puzzle is really about setting clear boundaries.

I find that successful *givers* tend to be specialists rather than generalists. What I mean by that is they focus on giving in a particular way they feel is aligned with their interests and their expertise. That way, if you love making connections, for example, focus your giving on doing lots of introductions and giving. If that's your focus, it becomes pretty energizing and efficient for you as opposed to distracting and exhausting.

Successful *givers* aren't necessarily alturistic. Instead, they try to integrate their desire to help others with their own goals and ambitions.

It's interesting, because that brings up a really clear point: although being a *giver* has a self-interest, it is an enlightened self-interest, because it doesn't just benefit the individual. In your book, you offer some advice on this mannerism: *help generously, and without thought of return, but also ask often for what you need.* **It seems that a successful *giver* also has to be very clear about what they're looking for. Would that be a correct assumption?**

Yeah, that's exactly right. I think one of the biggest surprises when we look at this data is that successful *givers* are also successful help-seekers. The *givers* who fail are the ones who are never willing to ask other people for support when they need it.

I've encountered *givers*, who are just uncomfortable asking for help. Part of that is something we all feel, which is we don't want to be helpless or incompetent or dependent. But for a *giver* there's an extra challenge, which is you like to be on the giving end of every exchange. You don't want to be a burden to anyone else. I always like to joke with a *counter-giver* who won't ask for something. For example, I'll say: *Kevin, if you're one of those people, if you never ask then you're depriving the people in your life of the opportunity to give.*

I think that, fundamentally, there is a distinction between taking and receiving. A lot of *givers* don't want to ask, because they don't want to be *takers*. A *taker* is somebody who uses someone else for sole personal gain, whereas a receiver is somebody who says: *"Look, I often enjoy giving, but in this situation you have something that I really need. I will accept your contribution, and then maintain a willingness to help out if I can in the future."*

A different form of reciprocity you mentioned earlier—and it's also prominent in your book—is referred to as 'paying it forward,' which is embedded in the idea of value-adding within a network. You give examples in your research of how this has been proven to be successful. But do you think it is widely effective and perhaps an important activity, this notion of 'paying it forward'?

I think it is. One of the most interesting habits that I've found among *givers* who are enormously productive is that they are actually able to convert *matchers* into *givers*, in a way that's intensified for everybody involved.

A simple example: one of my favorite characters in the book—whom I know you've had a lot fun learning about—is Adam Rifkin. Adam was named the best networker in the world by *Fortune* magazine, and just has an extraordinary number of connections that he's developed through everybody he meets. What Adam does, after he helps somebody, maybe it's two or three months later, he'll reach out to them and ask for a favor. You start to think, *"Well wait a minute, this guy's just a clever matcher. He's helping first and then he's asking for payback later."* Then he throws in a twist, which is, he's rarely asking for himself. Most of the time he's saying: *"Look, Kevin, I helped you out a couple of months ago. Now, I'm trying to help somebody else in a similar way. Would you be willing to help me help them?"*

A lot of the *matchers* he helped really want to pay it back to Adam, and the closest way that they can do that is to help him out with his efforts to help somebody different. What happens then is he's got this whole network of people who are willing to operate like *givers*. This means any time anyone in that network needs help, they can go to anybody else. Whereas, if you don't have that *pay it forward* mentality, you can only go to the people that you've directly traded favors with in the past.

Also, there must be another element to this. Some of your extensive research reveals that particular kinds of *givers* **are likely to become consistently more successful than maybe** *takers* **and** *matchers*. **Is this, in part, due to the rise of the sharing economy movement, or is there something more fundamental, or even more basic, at work?**

That's a great question. It's not one I have a good answer to, especially because I like to answer most of these kinds of questions with data. I haven't seen a good study yet about how the rise of the sharing economy has really affected the success of *givers*, or any broader patterns.

I think intuitively it's right. I think that as we have more mechanisms that allow people to share their time, their knowledge, their skills, even their homes, it's easier for people to recognize this idea that the *Harvard* professor Robert Putnam called 'generalized reciprocity.'

This basically states that direct reciprocity is sort of old school: *'you do something for me, I'll do something for you.'* Whereas generalized reciprocity is a little more complicated. It focuses more on: *'I'll do something for you without expecting anything back from you, but knowing that if I do that, somebody at some point is more likely to do something for me.'* I think that the sharing economy has really promoted a mentality that allows people to 'pay it forward' without necessarily expecting that immediate return but believing—if they model that kind of behavior—that kind of behavior will increase, and it will benefit everyone.

In your book you mention *FreeCycle*, **but also** *Airbnb* **and the** *Kahn Academy*. **And there's a whole bunch of businesses operating in this new sharing economy mentality. Would it be fair to say you're suggesting generosity—possibly in some cases altruism, maybe even humility—could be an effective business strategy?**

It sounds crazy, but yes! [Laughing] I think the qualifier I would throw in there is that I believe there's a time and a place where those strategies are effective and there are also circumstances where they're really dangerous. I think it's very rare to say that humility is *always* a good idea, that generosity is *always* a good idea.

I will say, though, that I'm balanced. People who adopt a giving mindset in the majority of their interactions end up finding that it brings lots of rewards with it. Not only conventional kinds of success but also greater meaning and purpose, and richer relationships.

I imagine the other side of this includes more significant hurdles, which a natural *giver* **would face, for example social and cultural norms and expectations, particularly in the business world. For example, after reading your book, a client of mine realized he was actually a** *giver* **pretending to be a** *taker* **simply due to the common perceptions around how we traditionally engage in business. It's this sort of difficulty, which societal norms place on** *givers*. **Do you think this is an accurate assessment and do you feel it is shifting dramatically at the moment?**

I do. But it's a complicated thing. I believe the norms vary a lot from one organization to another as well as across industries and national cultures. I'm surprised by the number of people who

I'm surprised by the number of people who tell me they hold *giver* values, but fear that if they express those values it's a sign of weakness.

tell me they hold *giver* values, but fear that if they express those values it's a sign of weakness. They basically leave these values behind once they walk into the office. They say: *"Look, I'm basically going to adopt a 'taking' or a 'matching' approach in most of my interactions. Then, every once in a while, I'll meet somebody who I realize has the same values and then they get to see the real me."*

I've encountered a lot of people who fit the description that you gave of your client. I think some of that comes from an idea—which is false—that success is zero sums, that for me to win you have to lose. I think some of it also comes from the fact there are a lot of former *givers* and *matchers* who have started acting like *takers* after getting burned one too many times and learning the hard way. They believe: *'Yeah, there are 'takers' out there and that means I need to be a little more cautious. If I don't put myself first, nobody else will."*

On the flip side of that, you assert that *takers* are also at risk—more so today—because your research suggests that, in our networked society, when people get burned by *takers*, they punish them by sharing reputation information and gossip that represents a widespread, efficient, low cost form of punishment. You also refer to this as a *'taker tax.'* Is social media simply leveling the playing field?

I believe it's certainly taking a step in that direction. It's harder today to be anonymous and invisible as a *taker* than it was before social media and also before the rise of highly collaborative teamwork and the growth of the service sector in most industrialized economies where most of us are more interdependent than we used to be. It's certainly a lot easier to track people's reputations now than it ever was before.

I think the reactions you're describing are most pronounced among *matchers*. *Matchers* really believe in a just world. If you're a *matcher*, you think that there should always be an 'eye for an eye.' When you see a *taker* act selfishly and get away with it, you as a *matcher* feel like it's your mission in life [laughter] to punish the heck out of that person.

I think the ability to keep track of those people on *LinkedIn* and *Facebook*, to figure out who else they know, to occasionally observe their behavior on *Twitter*, or to find out biographical information through a *Google* search, it does make it harder for *takers* to exploit one person without getting discovered by the next person.

[Laughing] It does seem very premeditated and strategic to chase someone down like that and punish them.

[Laughing] It does. I think that's a great source of joy for a true *matcher*.

Are you seeing this also apply to organizations, brands, and branding? Corporate Social Responsibility, which I think we could agree is sort of tokenism in many cases, is now being replaced by the more genuine or more significant Reputation Capital. In your opinion, is this impacting the number of good corporate citizens, or is that too simplistic?

I don't have a good sense of that. I would like to think that in general we've seen enough of a backlash toward Corporate Social Responsibility and cause-marketing initiatives that are just lip service, or that are done for purely instrumental reasons, that leaders are starting to figure out if they're going to do it, they need to do it right and it needs to mean something.

I think the jury is still out from my perspective, in terms of the evidence. There was a really nice study that Norbert Schwarz and his colleagues published a few years ago that looked at the effects of Corporate Social Responsibility on companies with bad reputations. For example, if you're a cigarette company what kind of impact do you provide when you start investing in a bunch of healthcare causes? [Laughing]

The finding was that, essentially, the more you promote those efforts, the more it backfires because people know you're just doing it to try to make up for the harm that you've done. But actual time and money invested in the activities themselves really paid off. The lesson there from these researchers was you should spend more time actually doing social responsibility and less time advertising it.

Perhaps a good example might be *McDonald's* where they've got the *Ronald McDonald House* for children with illnesses. The big contradiction there is that many people say that *McDonald's* is contributing to obesity and child health issues. But at the same time they're actively doing something real about trying to resolve some aspects of those conditions and illnesses. I guess that's probably one of the few case studies that I can think of that might somehow be walking the line with some success. Would you agree?

Yes. There's a really interesting question around this. In fact, there's actually some research on this by Anne Lewinsky and Joshua Margolis. They talk about necessary evils in organizations, the idea being: *"What happens when you do either a task, or are involved in a program that does harm, in the interest of the greater good?"*

Do the ends justify the means? I think that's a great question to ponder for *McDonald's*. Is it worth actually contributing to obesity, because you can generate enough revenue and enough awareness eventually perhaps to stop it? I don't know. Are they willing to put themselves out of business? It's a fascinating question.

I guess the question they would need to ask themselves is: do they want to put themselves out of their current business, but perhaps find a new business model that will be more satisfying, more rewarding and more beneficial to a lot more people? It goes back to that *giver* culture mentality you were talking about earlier, that it's just really a slight shift of goals and objectives that might actually give you a higher return in success, though maybe not in the short term. I know your research came up with—what is the phrase?—one person you quote says: *being a giver is not a 100-yard dash but it's invaluable in a marathon.* **In terms of shifting their business model it certainly wouldn't be a 100-yard dash for *McDonald's* to change immediately, but I'm sure if they were genuine about what they want to do, they could have a business model that would be equally as successful, maybe in a different way.**

I do think that's probably where we will see them move in the long run. We've all observed in the short run, the growth of healthier options on the menu. I think that is highly likely to continue.

And that's probably due to public pressure and cultural expectations, at least in industrialized countries.

Yes, I think that's part of the story. I've also been impressed by at least a few executives at *McDonald's* who have said: *"Look, part of my contribution to this organization is going to be pushing us toward doing what's right."*

I guess the extreme example, on the other hand, and you mention it in your book, is *Enron*. But, it's becoming increasingly difficult to be opaque today, as we discussed earlier. That said, *takers* also seek to adopt *giver* characteristics

in order to get what they want in the short term, possibly at the expense of others. We've discussed this a little bit, but how can you spot a *taker* in giver's clothing?

Well, I think that the first thing to do is contrast the idea of *givers* and *takers* with the personality trait of agreeableness. Agreeable people are people who typically come across as very warm and friendly and amiable, with disagreeable people being more challenging and critical and skeptical. Most of us stereotype agreeable people as *givers*, and disagreeable people as *takers*. Yet, I've found that you can actually plot those in a little 2 x 2 matrix, because you're agreeableness is basically your outer veneer. How you come across on the surface where if giving and taking are your inner motives, what are your real intentions toward others. That means, we have some people who are actually disagreeable *givers* who might be rough and tough and gruff but ultimately have others best interest at heart.

I know a few of those...

To your point, we need to watch out for the agreeable *takers*, those are the *takers* who create an aura of generosity but then ultimately are trying to only advance their own interests. There are a couple of different ways to spot truly agreeable *takers* in particular, one is a pattern that I've come to call, 'kissing up, kicking down,' which is something we see a lot.

The *takers* are typically trying to act generous when impressing powerful people, but find it's a lot of work to fake generosity in all of their interactions. They let their guard down a little bit when dealing with peers and subordinates. One implication is you might refer to somebody with the following attitude: *don't trust it as much if it comes from above, than if it comes from below.*

There are a few other tell-tale signs. When talking about their successes, *takers* tend to claim personal credit for collective achievements. They use more *I's* and *me's* instead of *us's* and *we's*. On the flip side, when they fail they're more likely to blame others.

One of my other favorite ways to spot a *taker* is not asking them what *they* would do in a situation but what they think *others* might do. Let's say this is a job interview setting. Rather than asking what would you do in this situation, Kevin, I would ask what you think 'other' people would do, because most of us tend to

The *takers* are typically trying to act generous when impressing powerful people, but find it's a lot of work to fake generosity in all of their interactions, for example when dealing with peers and subordinates.

project our motives onto others. There's integrity test research for example, suggesting that if you look at stealing, you can ask people: *"What percentage of employees do you think steal at least $10 worth of merchandise from their employers every year?"* The higher your guess, the greater the odds that you're a *taker*. This is an exercise which is great fun. You think about that question and you're like: *"Well, if I'm a 'taker,' I took $400 last year from my company, so probably a lot of people do that."* Whereas, the *givers* are like: *"Who would steal a tent?"*

[Laughing] Another insight in your book, which is of particular interest, relates to your suggestion that the size of a portrait photograph in an annual report can actually tell *givers* from *takers*. Can you expand on that discovery?

This is a brilliant study by Chatterjee and Hambrick. They listed over 100 tech companies. They got Wall Street analysts to rate the CEOs of those companies. It was basically a *taker* scale: how selfish, how egotistical, how narcissistic is each CEO?

Then they looked for clues that correlated with the analyst's ratings, and indeed, the CEOs who were rated as *takers* by the analysts had more prominent photographs of themselves in their company's annual reports. Their pictures were larger and they were more likely to be alone, sending a pretty clear signal that: *"I'm the most important person in this company. It's all about me."*

We can see those patterns in everyday life too. There's a recent study by Keith Campbell and a colleague, showing that on *Facebook*, you can actually spot the narcissistic *takers* by looking at how attractive they appear—how vain—in their profile photo. I like to point out here that the *takers* are not necessarily 'hotter' than the rest of us, in general, but you will find a bigger gap between their average photo and how good they look in the profile picture. They've got to put their best foot forward.

You'll have a whole rush of people now going to check their *Facebook* photo.

[Laughter]

Once again, it does come down to these perceptions, social norms and expectations. Not only in the business world but just in society, there seems to be a much more competitive attitude out there. When anyone is putting any kind of image

forward they want to make it look as best as possible. Of course, there are some who claim the people who obsessively use *Facebook* are narcissistic (or voyeuristic), so there is a societal cultural shift happening anyway. Does that muddy the waters, or is it simply that people who are a bit vain might also be quite generous?

I've long been interested in tracking another huge but related area, which is: do you, in your profile, show a picture of yourself with the most important person you've ever met, thereby trying to get status by association?

I think it's fair to say that not all narcissists are *takers*. There's such a thing as a narcissistic *giver*. I've encountered it from time to time when people will claim that they're better at helping others than anybody else: *"I am the most generous person you'll ever meet."*

That's a contradiction in terms.

In a way, that's right! Some of these people are really passionate about helping others and that's what their ego is invested in. They have an inflated sense of their own generosity and importance in helping others.

For the most part, I find a very strong correlation between narcissism and *taking*. One of the tale-tell signs of many narcissists is that they have fragile and inflated egos because they believe that they have to be better than others in order to succeed.

That doesn't necessarily muddy the waters, but it does get tricky when you're trying to spot *takers* and *givers*. Something that comes to mind is, when looking at the complexities of what we're talking about, it could become hard work for people to either spot *takers* and *givers*, but also to decide whether they themselves are a *taker* or a *giver*. You would want all this to be a very natural, free-flowing, organic way of being. How then can someone transform themselves after realizing they've been living a *taker* behavioral life for a long time, for reasons that are perhaps external—for example, how they were brought up, or places they've worked; whatever. But they come to this realization and they want to move towards being a *giver*. I know we're generalizing, but is that something they have to work at, or would you say it needs to be a more natural shift?

It could actually go both ways. I think one of the easiest ways to shift your style is to recognize that we all tend to become more giving when we're really passionate about something. If you were to think about your favorite topic to read about, or a hobby that you really love, it's really hard *not* to share that with other people. In fact, sometimes, you cross the boundary from giving to just annoying people, because you're so into something.

I think focusing on things that you really love, is one of the easiest ways to become a little more giving. My other favorite step is something I learned, again from Adam Rifkin, who I mentioned earlier. Adam says if you want to be a *giver*, you don't want to be Mother Theresa or Gandhi. That's not sustainable for most of us. Rather, you should try to do a few more 'five-minute favors' every week.

Adam will say: *"Look, there are a lot of ways that you can add high value to other people's lives at a low personal cost. For example, making an introduction, writing a little recommendation or a note of gratitude to somebody else."* He's got a whole list of favours that I think the easiest deliverance step is to say: *"I'm going to pick a few people that I would like to add more value to, and try to figure out how—in just a few minutes—I could make their life a little bit better."*

I think there's another important point here: a *giver* needs to manage their time because, as you said earlier, you don't want to be one of those unsuccessful *givers* where you're doing everything for everyone and all of a sudden you don't have any time to do what you need to do. You need to edit or curate who you are able to best add value to. Is that what Adam is suggesting?

Yes, I think that's exactly right. In a way Adam is thinking about return on investment: *"Where could I give effectively that's going to allow me to have the most impact?"* That doesn't necessarily always involve the greatest investment of time.

If I remember correctly from reading your book, I think Adam actively asks people to *pay it forward* as well. He doesn't consider it as an assumption. He actually asks people.

He does.

I think focusing on things that you really love, is one of the easiest ways to become a little more giving.

Could this also be part of coaching *givers* to become more strategic about how they spend their time? For example, if a successful *giver* keeps reminding people: *"Make sure you pay this forward,"* **just as one little tip, because this has a ripple effect and helps that person understand how giving can actually add value.**

I think it's useful in that way. It's also probably a pretty good screening mechanism for figuring out what the other people in your network are—*giver, matcher* or *taker*. This is something that I've been doing more often lately. For example, when somebody asks me whether I know somebody who can help with a particular request, or if I have the contact to a certain organization where they're looking for a job, what I will often do is send them the contact information but let them reach out independently, and allow them to just use my name. Then I get a pretty independent view into whether that person is genuinely willing to help.

Whereas, when I make the introduction, usually people will follow through and I don't then know if it's because they genuinely enjoy giving or because they're just trying to match something that I've given to them in the past. I like letting people give in a more naturalistic, spontaneous experience. And this helps me figure out whether somebody's going to pay it forward or not.

You probably also spot those who are just being opportunistic because, again, it moves closer to *matcher* **or even** *taker* **where they're leveraging a connection with someone—but purely for their own ends.**

That's right.

It might prompt people to consider how they operate in a network, being very conscious of what they do and that could lead to a little bit of paranoia. It's funny: In your book you touch on paranoia. Particularly the highly competitive world where there is paranoia, for example in the business world. But this can also influence behavior and action. The distinguished psychologist Brian Little poses a compelling opposite—*pronoia: 'the delusional belief that other people are applauding your well-being or saying nice things about you behind your back.'*

Humorous and interesting as that is, you suggest it may be a reality for *givers*, rather than a delusion. Does this go back to Reputation Capital, which we discussed earlier?

Yes, I think it does. I've enjoyed the idea that perhaps we could envision a world where we had more *givers* and instead of worrying that people were out to get you [laughter] you could worry that they were out to help you. I think, at some level, if that's the fear you're creating, it does have a lot of reputational benefits with people trying to figure out: *'why is this person conspiring to help me?'* [laughter]

The other thing that I find interesting about the *pronoia* concept is that the only reason it can exist is because people are either skeptical by disposition or they've had some experience to suggest that when others help they probably have some ulterior motives. The idea that when somebody tries to help, one might immediately begin to think: *"What's really going on here?"*...

What's the agenda?..

Yes. I think this suggests that somebody's probably been surrounded by too many *takers*. One thing we can probably all do more effectively is figure out who the *givers* and *matchers* are around us and create a little community of people that we can trust.

I guess another way is to be much more relaxed about it. If you do get burned, just say: *"Okay, I'm not going to chase them down and issue a 'taker tax.' I'm just going to quietly shift away and never interact with them again."* **It's more about surrounding ourselves with people we have a natural affinity with, as opposed to overanalyzing it...**

I think it's very tempting to become almost overly scientific about this. I could start keeping track of all the cues [laughter] that lead me to think that somebody has one style or another. A lot of it is going to be based on intuition and gut feeling and everyday experience. I think it's reasonable to treat the sense of trust you have with somebody else as a proxy for what their style might be.

Personally, on a rare occasion, my natural instinct might be to try and pursue a *taker* for whatever reason. But generally, my thinking would be I'd rather spend that time doing

something more meaningful or helping somebody else rather than interacting with this person who I feel just burnt me. I prefer to just step away. I think that might be, at least in my experience, a way of trying to not make this too scientific, not make this too onerous.

On a deeper level, there are a lot of cues you talk about but which could make people feel this is a lot of hard work. However, over time, you suggest just having a few things on your radar can keep you focused. Otherwise, it should be a very natural way of living. Would that be a good assessment?

Yes, I think that's a great summary, actually.

With that in mind, do you foresee a genuine, mainstream, even sustained corporate *giver* culture any time soon?

I've certainly been excited by some organizations taking steps in this direction. How widely will it spread? For me, this is an open question. But I think there are many organizations working on doing a better job of screening out *takers*, of redefining performance to not just include individual accomplishments but also the impact of your success on other people, to really create norms that make it acceptable to ask, so that *givers* know who could benefit from their help and how. I'd love to see more of those practices spread.

With that in mind, Kevin, let me turn this around on you and ask: if you were going to build an organization that really operated with a culture of giving, what are a few of the steps you'd recommend from your experience?

I think one of the key things I feel is very current—but also very close to me—is a culture of collaboration. That's not just because everyone has a voice. It means if you're involved, we expect to hear from you. I genuinely feel—and I've said this for many years—whether you're a student or a high performing executive, you have some life experience, some outlook on the world, and you have an opinion. That's all valid. It doesn't really matter about seniority. It really relies on your experience. That's the first thing I would establish.

I think there are many organizations working on doing a better job of screening out *takers*, of redefining performance to not just include individual accomplishments but also the impact of your success on other people.

The other thing—which I also actively pursue—is to try and do things that are meaningful. I don't just mean not-for-profit or charity, though that could be part of it, but that your service or product isn't just another widget or another 'thing' to do. We must constantly remind ourselves that we turn up to work every day, 10 hours a day. We sit with people. We need to like the people we're sitting with and we've got to feel like we're contributing something meaningful—at least in our understanding of what's meaningful.

I believe these are the two cornerstones, which I'd start with. And I actively strive to do this in my own business. I'm not sure if that clearly answers your question, but that's how I would at least start, and then pursue.

Great! A related question that I was curious about, since you've implemented some of these ideas and shared them with other people in your network: what have people been most surprised by?

First of all, it is clear there's terminology around all this. The client I mentioned earlier; I don't think he was even aware there was a way of looking at splitting up personas between *giver, taker* and *matcher*. All of a sudden, a light bulb was turned on in his mind and it allowed him to reshape and refocus his natural characteristics and be comfortable in his own skin. That's one of the first clear things I've witnessed.

In terms of my own experience, I think it's probably made me a little more aware of whom the *takers* might be. My own fear—and a fear I've heard from other people—is the unsuccessful *giver*, the person who naturally wants to help people but really feels like: *"Why the hell aren't I getting anywhere? I'm helping everyone. I've got to just stop this. I've got to stop giving so much."* **As opposed to:** *"I've got to stop giving in the way [laughs] that I've been giving."* **I think that's another light bulb moment for people.**

Then, at the higher end, what I'm hearing, and this is only at the early stages... [Pause] I'm working with a client with offices around the world. The person I gave your book to is a senior manager, and I think they are looking at—as you said earlier—encouraging the quiet achievers, those people who get a lot done but they do so by helping others. I think this

senior manager is becoming more aware and asking herself: *"How can we celebrate this behaviour—for them and for the company? How can we generate incentives?"*

The greatest insight, which I've gotten from your book, is that it provides a framework for issues people may not have been naturally able to identify within themselves. They may in some cases have been uncomfortable with being burned too many times but still want to give.

That's such an exciting way to think about these ideas.

Kevin, you've obviously demonstrated your style in all the time and effort you put into actually modeling this behavior and trying to encourage others to adopt it as well.

I think it has given me a framework. Giving is something I am naturally inclined towards, simply because I enjoy helping people. Not because I want to get a return on it. I just didn't think I was being as effective as I could be. The ideas in your book really helped put some frameworks around this. But in a way that can be maintained; in a way that's natural; that's not forced; that's genuine and not just: *"I should do this because it'll be a good thing to do."*

Although all this must be natural I also realised from your book these frameworks are rather scientific—research-driven. In saying that, one can't operate as a person with all of this criteria needing to be 'ticked off' every day. It has to be a real, genuine, authentic characteristic and behaviour. Once you know that, then you work on it, you can—as Adam Rifkin says— focus and be more strategic about how you can best add value and how you can best help people.

The 'five-minute' favour activity, which Adam Rifkin suggests, has also influenced how I might see a quick way to help people or introduce somebody. Even on *LinkedIn,* **where it is easy to recommend or endorse someone. It's really simple. It's the little things.**

Excellent!

One can't operate as a person with all of this criteria needing to be 'ticked off' every day. It has to be a real, genuine, authentic characteristic and behaviour.

Thinking to create value

Kevin Finn in conversation with Edward de Bono

Kevin Finn: Can you describe, in simple terms, the essence of your approach to thinking?

Edward de Bono: My approach to thinking is based on an understanding of how the brain works. In my medical research I dealt a lot with the complicated systems of the body—glands, kidneys, circulation, everything. I developed theories of self-organizing systems and applied these to the neural networks of the brain. My book *"The Mechanism of Mind,"* published in 1969, describes this. To put it simply, the brain works as a self-organizing system; it forms patterns. So I explored the question: *"What is a logical patterning system?"* From that, I developed my approach to thinking.

In your book *Lateral Thinking* you place a great deal of importance on design. Is this because design is a deliberate act and aligns well with how we should think?

Yes. I put a lot of importance on design, because design is putting together what you have to deliver, in terms of the values you want or provide. Most of our thinking at all levels—school, university, everything—is concerned with *analysis*. Analysis is concerned with finding the truth: *"What is this?"* Design, on the other hand, is producing something which isn't there, or wasn't there before. Indeed, there's a huge problem with our thinking in general and at all levels, including at senior levels. The problem relates to a belief that our thinking is concerned with finding the truth. This began in *The Middle Ages*, where schools, universities, and general thinking were all in the hands of the Church. The Church was interested in finding *the truth*, in order to prove heretics wrong and to support their belief structure.

So we developed good thinking—finding *the truth*—which became scientific thinking, which is excellent. But culturally, we never developed thinking for creating value.

So, how do we need to think to produce something that doesn't yet exist? Design is one particular aspect of that because it concerns itself with creating something that doesn't yet exist, as opposed to finding *the truth*, which is always there until we find it.

I put a lot of importance on design, because design is putting together what you have to deliver, in terms of the values you want or provide.

In your work, you often refer to breaking patterns of traditional thinking. Since design is a very deliberate act, is it correct to say your work seeks to promote and prompt people to think deliberately?

Yes, certainly. That's why the Chinese are very interested in my work, because they know they need creativity. They're not going to be creative by being crazy or 'off the wall.' They like a sensible, structured approach to creativity, so they like my books and training programmes.

You also place considerable importance on creativity. In your book *Lateral Thinking* **you state:** *"In order to be able to use creativity one must rid it of this aura of mystique and regard it as a way of using the mind—a way of handling information."* **I understand you have been criticized for not offering a definition for creativity. Why are you reluctant to define creativity?**

Our general approach to creativity is a belief that it's not normal, that it's mysterious, that it's some strange talent that only certain people have, but most people don't have and there's nothing you can do about it except find people who are creative. That is so ridiculous.

I look at creativity as an activity of the brain, an activity with patterned systems. Interestingly, the most important function of the brain, which amazingly philosophers have never mentioned and psychologists pay very little attention to, if any, is *humour*, because humor indicates the brain is working as a patterning system.

Here is a simple example: A man aged 90 dies and goes down to hell. As he's wandering around, he sees a friend, also aged 90. His friend has a beautiful young lady sitting on his knee. So, he says to his friend: *"Are you sure this is hell, because you seem to be having rather a good time?"* His friend looks up and says: *"It's hell all right. I'm the punishment for her."*

[Laughing]

This demonstrates a pattern, a perfectly logical pattern heading towards an end-point. But then a different end-point is introduced, which in hindsight is perfectly logical. If the

Our general approach to creativity is a belief that it's not normal, that it's mysterious, that it's some strange talent that only certain people have... That is so ridiculous.

brain can do that, then there's an absolute need for creativity because there are points in the brain, which you cannot get to with logic, but once you're there they are perfectly logical in hindsight. So without creativity you're never going to get to those points, meaning humor is very, very key—and, as I said, it's totally neglected.

Now, with regards to offering a definition of creativity, the problem with creativity in the English language is that it's so wide. It covers artistic creativity, intellectual creativity, etc.

I would define creativity as developing an idea—or project, or product, or whatever it is—which in hindsight is valuable and logical but which you could not have gotten there by logical development. In hindsight, yes, but not with foresight. So, it's the asymmetry of patterns that defines creativity.

You believe: *"Insight, creativity and humour are so elusive because the mind is so efficient."* **You go on to describe how this is based on patterns and the objective is to re-pattern the mind. But is this easier said than done? Are we simply hard-wired to resist change?**

Now the brain, of course, is designed to use patterns, otherwise life would be incredibly difficult. If you get up in the morning and have 11 pieces of clothing to put on, there are actually over 39 million possible ways of getting dressed. If you tried one every minute of your waking life, you would need to live to be 76 years old doing nothing else except trying ways of getting dressed. So clearly, we should be immensely grateful that the brain establishes routine patterns and uses them.

In general, for almost all our activities, we should be very grateful that the brain does use patterns. But then we also need to find ways of escaping from these patterns, and that is what I'm talking about.

I love the audacity of the opening line in the preface of your book *Six Thinking Hats***:** *"The Six Thinking Hats method may be the most important change in human thinking for the past twenty-three hundred years."* **You go on to qualify:** *"That may seem a rather exaggerated claim, but the evidence is beginning to point that way."* **The evidence**

you refer to relates to major corporations like *IBM*, *Siemens* and *Statoil*, who have implemented your methods with great success. Successful outcomes are an obvious benefit to business, but can you share with us some of the tangible benefits businesses can expect from employing your thinking methods?

Yes, yes. I often say *Six Thinking Hats* may be the most important change in human thinking for the past twenty-three hundred years, because it relates to practical thinking. I say this because of the *Greek gang of three* (Socrates, Plato and Aristotle), whom twenty-three or twenty-four hundred years ago developed logical argument. Again, because of the influence of the Church, we were very happy with logical argument, and we base everything on logical argument whether it's law courts, parliament, whatever.

So we have that, and it is excellent, but it's not sufficient. *Argument* is all about proving your case, so the use of the mind is entirely negative. Technically, it's simply defending your point of view.

Now, the brain works according to its mood, and there are many other possible moods in the brain, which we never use, for example the constructive mood, the creative mood, and so on. The *Six Thinking Hats* allows every person at the meeting to use their brain fully, not just for attacking.

What is really interesting—and contrary to expectations—you might think if people use their brain so much more thoroughly in all the different aspects—emotional, creative, etc—then it should take longer to resolve things. Right? In fact, it takes one tenth of the time. A major American bank claimed that using *Six Thinking Hats* reduced their meeting times to one tenth of what it normally took.

The reason is that, in *argument*, everyone wants to exert their ego in any little point they pick up to be negative and this produces endless little negative arguments. Whereas, with *Six Thinking Hats* there is a requirement to be constructive. You have to move something forward. Of course, the *Black Hat* is there to criticize and to be critical, but that's only one of the *Six Thinking Hats*.

The *Six Thinking Hats* has had many successful outcomes. I once worked with a company, which experienced a lot of staff strikes. They used *Six Thinking Hats* to reduce the number of strikes to around one quarter of what they had been.

Another example: when *Nokia* started making mobile phones, they invited me to Helsinki right at the beginning of this transition. At the time it was a timber company making paper—specializing in lavatory paper, I think. I began by talking to a whole group, approximately 70 people. They listened, and they developed *Nokia* to become the biggest suppliers of mobile phones in the world.

So your work and your thinking tools are a catalyst for change?

Yes. Of course in the case of *Nokia*, the advantage was that they were entering into a new area so they didn't have established ideas, or an established business. Of course, this could be interpreted in a different way.

Some might say they were successful because they had a clear idea, which is why they invited me in the first place. This is possible.

In your words: *"Culture is concerned with establishing ideas. Education is concerned with communicating those ideas. Both are concerned with improving ideas and bringing them up to date. The only available method for changing ideas is conflict."* **Educators like Sir Ken Robinson, and more recently Salman Khan of the Khan Academy, also believe the one-size-fits-all approach to traditional education is incredibly limited and, like you, they prefer a more creative, self-paced approach to learning. In your opinion, is the traditional education system too big, too conservative and too business-oriented to change—is there too much at stake? To use your own terms, is this the difference between the perceived 'rightness' and 'richness' of education?**

The problem with education is it believes it has a responsibility to teach youngsters about the way the world is. But even in that, I think it is deficient.

For instance, in some countries like the United Kingdom, a great deal of time is spent on history—*the Tudors, the War of the Roses*, etc—but no time at all is spent on the *"now story."* Current education doesn't really focus on how the world works today, how business works, how employment works, how government works. So youngsters may leave school knowing all about history, but not much (if anything) about the world today. That's one problem.

I believe the business of education is to teach children how the world works. But generally speaking, the impression is that the role of education isn't to develop the full potential of the skills of children, particularly in relation to skills they would need to improve the world. This is missing. Although, when schools teach my thinking skills tools, it shows significant improvement in all other subjects—between 30 and 100 percent in all other subjects.

When we look at the world today—with continued financial instability, increasingly volatile conflict zones and the real threat of climate change—one would sense our society might have *thinking deficiency*. **But how can these immense and sticky situations achieve better outcomes, considering all the cultural, economic, societal and political nuances involved?**

Now, the problem with our regular thinking—and again, this applies to many areas, and universities in particular—is that the approach is on *analysis*. In a way, this is caveman thinking. When a caveman comes out of a cave, and he sees a red object in the bushes, what is his thinking? He's thinking: *"What is this? Is this an apple, which is good to eat? Is it a poison or something dangerous? Is it something I don't know?"* In other words, his thinking relies on recognition.

Take a doctor in a clinic. They see a patient. The doctor examines the patient. They do some tests. What are they looking for? They are looking to identify a standard situation so that they can then apply a standard treatment.

Virtually all our thinking in school—and thereafter—is to analyze, to find the standard situation, to provide the standard answer. Of course, there's nothing wrong with that. It's very useful, but it's not sufficient. That's why we find it difficult to make changes.

It is widely accepted that you are the original innovator and pioneer of new thinking approaches. We now see the emergence of many thinking-oriented approaches, for example *Design Thinking*, **which have led to successful business enterprises based on these thinking concepts. We could confidently argue this trend might not be possible if not for your work. But does this trend encourage you, or are you concerned in any way?**

Virtually all our thinking in school—and thereafter—is to analyze, to find the standard situation, to provide the standard answer. That's why we find it difficult to make changes.

Yes, obviously, I started writing about these things in 1970. Since then, there have been many other approaches. Some of them are based on my works. Some of them are inspired by my work. Some of them are just co-incidental.

Would this trend have been possible without my work? It's impossible to tell, but I think that my work has had a big influence on the whole trend happening at the moment. I hear from many different fields—people in music and art, among many other areas— about how my work has affected them. Of course, I am concerned about people who—as it were—steal my work and claim it's theirs. That's a problem.

But are you encouraged by the general sense that a focus on thinking is becoming more mainstream?

Yes, yes, I am.

When we spoke yesterday you mentioned a new book you're writing—and which is yet to be published. You have recently turned 82, a wonderful achievement in itself. You are still developing ideas and material, but what do you believe will be the legacy of your life's work?

My new book will be about *'thinking to create value'* because, as I say, the Church was only interested in finding *'the truth.'*

Thinking to create value, which I call *'bonting'*—a word that comes from the Latin *'bonus'* and *'bonum,'* and of course, my name de Bono. Lets say we are sitting at a meeting and we are analyzing figures, and so on. We could say: *"Wait a minute. Let's do some bonting. Let's create some value."* Because creating value is important.

I think the legacy of my life work centers around attention to deliberate direct thinking, both in terms of lateral thinking, and creativity, as well as the *Six Thinking Hats*, and aspects like that. They're very different from just the analysis of philosophers who were looking at things and putting names on concepts, and so and so.

Even though you're working on new a book *"Bonting"*, is it a correct assessment to suggest your work has always been about creating value?

The problem with education is it believes it has a responsibility to teach youngsters about the way the world is. But even in that, I think it is deficient.

Yes, that's absolutely true. It is the creation of value which doesn't yet exist, rather than the discovery of truth. I'm not saying discovery of truth is wrong. It's excellent, but it's not enough. That's why, a few years ago, I invented the word *Ebne, (Excellent But Not Enough)*.

[Both Laughing]

You might clean the floor, and may have done an excellent job—but not enough. We've also needed that word for twenty-four thousand years—since the *Greek gang of three*. Previously, we couldn't have added it because, if on the other side of the dialectic is *'truth'*, well, if someone was true, you can't be more true than the truth, right? It had to do with action operations.

The other side of the dialectic is perhaps good wasn't enough, and it would be very wrong to say, *"It's fine,"* when it's not. But it would be very wrong to say, *"It's wrong and bad,"* when it's not wrong and bad. So we *do* need a way of saying, *"It is excellent but not enough."*

And when you bring in *'truth,'* there is always the possibility of fanaticism—those people who will not budge because their belief is embedded in a particular truth...

Yes, that's right! And because with the truth, there's all the religious connotations; fanaticism means you can't consider other possibilities. So, my work is about value, rather than truth. That's not to say I think that the search for truth is wrong. It is correct, it's excellent—but it's not enough.

The language of culture, happiness and hostility

Kevin Finn in conversation with Dan Everett.

Kevin Finn: Over 30 years ago you went to a remote corner of the Brazilian Amazon as a Christian missionary to convert the *Pirahã*, a tribe of around 400 people. Remarkably, they converted you. How did they manage to do this? What was so powerful, so compelling about their beliefs and way of life that it made you an atheist?

Dan Everett: The first thing you have to do as a Christian missionary is tell people they have a savior. But in the case of the *Pirahã*, it just wasn't clear that they had anything to be saved from. Of course, one can talk about the problems of sickness, etc, but I've described the *Pirahã* as a very peaceful people, and that's correct. But everybody has exceptions, every society has exceptions.

Overall, the people were just very laid back, self sufficient and happy, and it made very little sense for me to start telling them they were lost, except from the theological perspective. But as I thought about it more, there were two things that really profoundly affected me. The first was this contentment and happiness, which I witnessed, but also their demand for evidence. If I told them something about Jesus, they expected that I had actually seen Jesus. That I had real direct evidence from the things that I was talking about. Otherwise, I wouldn't talk to them about it, right?

They came to me once and asked: *"Hey, Dan. Is Jesus brown like us or is he white like you?"* I said, *"Well, some people say he was brown and some people say he was white."*

To which they replied: *"But you saw him, so what was he?"* I said, *"Well, I've never talked to him."* They said: *"Well, your father must have seen him."* *"No, my father never saw him."* *"Well, who saw him?"* The answer, of course, was, *"I know of no one who's ever seen him."* For them, it just didn't make any sense.

As I thought about that, and considering I was not a Christian all my life, these things really made me reflect on the people and on the mission that I had gone there to carry out. It just didn't seem to make a lot of sense for me to continue to try to *'missionize'* them. More importantly, as I looked around and saw a lot of Christians—in churches in the United States, in churches in Brazil, in the missionary group that I was with, and many other contexts—I really didn't see anybody that was living a life I thought was any better than the *Pirahã*. These things all made me eventually go down a series of questions and answers that led me to abandon my faith.

From an objective point of view it seems to suggest you were somehow enlightened by their questions. And, on the other hand, the *Pirahã* are actually quite scientific about how they approach things, that they look for the evidence.

Yes, they are very empirical.

Was there a long time frame in which you changed, or was it a very abrupt change?

It was a long time frame. It started in the early 80s. It took about 20 years for me to come around to say that I, really, don't believe anymore. The consequences, if you're a missionary, of saying that you don't believe are unemployment and loss of relationships. It's not something you do lightly. 20 years may seem like a long time, but whenever I would doubt, I would try very hard not to doubt.

That's self preservation, I guess?

Yeah.

Many would argue that language preserves culture. Although the *Pirahã* have recently begun to learn Portuguese, they generally only speak their own language, which I believe, is unusual among Amazonian tribes. You're one of the few people who speak *Pirahã* fluently. One of the most fascinating aspects about the *Pirahã* language is how it can be communicated; their language can be spoken, hummed, sung, or whistled. How is it possible to sing and hum a language?

The reason that it's easier for the *Pirahã* to do this is that their language is tonal. The pitches on the vowels, whether the vowel is a high pitch or a low pitch, are very easy to whistle. When you combine that with the syllable structure of the language, and the general intonation and a number of other characteristics that use pitch, and length and loudness, you're able to whistle an entire phrase. They can follow you fine without context. They can communicate anything by whistling, or humming or these other ways that we can with consonants and vowels.

They can communicate anything by whistling, or humming.

Amazing! Can you yourself hum, whistle or sing the *Pirahã* language, or just speak it?

I speak it well, but I don't do those other things very well. If I do, they laugh. They think it's funny that I'm doing this. If they start whistling or humming, they can lose me very easily, very quickly.

[Laughing] I believe the *Pirahã* don't have any words for colours or numbers, and they don't have any words for past or future tense. Research from *MIT* suggests the *Pirahã* are the only culture in the world without numeracy. Aside from being a fascinating fact, is there a deeper significance to those findings?

Yes. I've tried to explain all of this based on a single principle that I've called the, *Immediacy of Experience Principle*. There's a very long, and involved and technical explanation of how this works. But the simple form of it is that they don't generalize more than they absolutely have to. Numbers are generalizations. It's not crucial to generalize like that so they simply don't. It goes beyond the things they experience.

For example, lets take *white*. White is an abstraction. Black is an abstraction. We call lots of things white: if you put all of them next to each other, they're not exactly the same colour. For the *Pirahã*, they describe things as they see them. *"This is clear." "This is clean." "This looks like water." "This looks like a leaf"* —in terms of colour.

In terms of numbers, it's also an abstraction to say *three potatoes* versus *three fish*. In other words, you've got this characteristic, "three", which goes beyond my experience. It applies to a range of possible circumstances they haven't yet experienced.

That said, they can generalize. They have the word *dog*, which refers to *all* dogs. That's a generalization. It's not that they don't generalize. It's that they don't generalize more than communication absolutely requires of them.

It's pretty efficient, and pretty economical.

Yeah. It's a very economical language, in that sense and in terms of the range of things they talk about, and the shortness of their sentences. Things are more concrete in some senses.

Of course, spoken language is integral to identity, but how important is visual language, considering the *Pirahã* have no words for colours? Do they have a particular visual language?

They have gestures, but they don't represent things in two dimensional space except for stick figures. They don't do drawings. They rarely do things like diagram maps on the ground. *"You go here and I'll go there"*—they don't represent things that way.

Their spoken language is very important. Their gestures are very important. Everything around them is mapped to an internal map. They not only know the jungle very well, but every part of the jungle has names. You wonder how they give can each other such precise directions to go places when they can't say: *"The third turn at the third path, or turn at the second river you come to."* They don't say things like that. But everything, every body of water, every path, all of these things have names. They can tell each other, with great precision, where to be. But it requires that their local environment is almost completely memorized and mapped in everyone's head.

Again, that's pretty amazing. One of the most unusual aspects of the *Pirahã* language is its grammar. It seems to challenge what is believed to be a fundamental rule of human language, which is *recursion*. Can you explain recursion in brief detail?

Recursion is a mathematical computational concept and one could get quite complicated with it. If you see a *matryoshka* doll——a Russian doll where one small doll goes inside a slightly larger doll, which goes inside a slightly larger doll—then that's recursion. That's putting one thing inside another thing of the same type.

In essence, it relates to taking a word and putting it with another word to form a larger word. Take the word *"truckdriver."* *"Truckdriver"* is made up of the word *"truck"* and the word *"drive."* But it's bigger than that. Putting the two words together makes this third word. I have a word *"truckdriver"* that has two smaller words, *"truck"* and *"drive"* inside it. That's recursion.

Equally, I can say: *"John's house."* That's a noun phrase with a possessor and a thing possessed. I can say: *"John's house,"* or I can say: *"John's brother's House."* Or: *"John's brother's, sister's, mother's, father-in-law's, cousin's house."* Those are all putting one noun phrase inside of another. Those are all recursion.

Another example, I can say: *"John spoke,"* or I can say: *"John said that Mary spoke,"* in which Mary spoke is a sentence inside the larger sentence: *"John said that."*

The ability to do this enables us to pack a lot of information into single sentences, when you start getting nouns that are recursive, inside phrases that are recursive, inside sentences that are recursive.

In a 2001 paper, Noam Chomsky [who is interviewed in Open Manifesto #4], Marc Hauser and Tecumseh Fitch said that recursion is the fundamental biological foundation for language that *only* humans have. However, *Pirahã* doesn't seem to have any evidence for recursion in the grammar like this. They can *think* recursively, which is an interesting story. And it's possible to see this when they tell a long story; you'll get one idea inside of another idea. That's thinking recursively, but it isn't grammatically recursive.
They could say something

like: *"Once upon a time,"* and then everything that follows is part of this larger story. But it's not part of the grammar. The fact that *Pirahã* lacks that characteristic drew a lot of attention to the language. And there have been a lot of experiments done.

The experimenters—who feature in the film *The Grammar of Happiness*—Ted Gibson and Steve Piantadosi, both at *MIT*, are actively, finally, finishing a paper to prove this. It should be out before too long.

This paper will be backed up with over 200 pages of text, the very text that they were analyzing in the film. This will be presented publicly. Why is that important? This is independent confirmation—if, of course they agree with me about the things that I have been arguing for, which is that recursion cannot be the basis of human language. In all my work over the last couple of years, I have argued that language is created in part by our culture. You can never understand any grammar unless you understand the culture in which it's embedded.

Why is that so radical?

I have argued that language is created in part by our culture. You can never understand any grammar unless you understand the culture in which it's embedded.

For the average non-linguist, that's not radical because it makes common sense. And I think that it's right. People would say things like: *"This culture raises cattle, therefore their language looks like this."* Or: *"This culture eats sushi so their language looks like this."* They put the object before the verb.

But there are a lot of silly claims out there. And linguists spent a lot of time showing how these weren't really precise claims and that they didn't make a lot of sense. The received wisdom, after a period of time, among all linguists and even many anthropologists, was that it had been decisively shown that culture and language were entirely separate except for words. Sure, there's a word for *haggis* in Scots Gaelic. But there's not a word for 'haggis' in Portuguese unless you use the actual word 'haggis' because Brazilians don't eat haggis. Nobody denied that. But many people, most people even, still deny that there's a greater link to culture in language than just the words.

I've just tried to show that—sure—those original arguments and some of things that people say were slightly left field. But there are a lot of other ways to look at this, not just in terms of the words, but in terms of how we talk. What do we talk about? How do we relate to one another? How long do we expect sentences to be? All of these things can be shown to link to culture, and it does give you a picture that language is partially shaped by culture. And at the same time, language shapes culture.

I've called it a 'symbiosis'; each one forms the other. It's not a chicken or egg problem. You start learning language on its own, you start learning culture on its own. Babies learn culture from the time they're in the womb. At some point, the learning of culture and learning of language come together. When you go to school, you're taught a lot about your culture through language.

You're also taught it through the ways that your friends dress, the things that they eat, the way they smell, the way they relate to one another, how much they touch one another. Those are all very important parts of culture. How long does one person talk? How long is considered polite for one person to talk? What are the kinds of relationships that determine how conversation will be structured? These are just things that are absorbed in their cultural values.

One of your greatest frustrations is the lack of scientific attitude towards your work. There doesn't seem to be a proper exchange of ideas in this particular issue, which one would actually expect from universities and science. What are they afraid of?

There are two things. On a personal level, people are irritated that anybody gets any—or a lot—of publicity. That seems to be some human issue, because everybody thinks their work is important. And it is! But they wonder why *you* get publicity, and they don't. Although this is one reason, it has nothing to do with the scientific debate. But it's a real factor in some of the anger.

The other issue is the significance [Noam] Chomsky has with a lot of people, because of his political and linguistic views. Chomsky said: *"All people have X,"* in recursion. I come along and say, *"These people [the Pirahã] don't have X."* There are two conclusions you could draw from that. One, Chomsky is wrong, or I'm wrong—or I'm saying that the *Pirahã* aren't humans. Since Chomsky says: *"All people have X,"* therefore, I must be saying the *Pirahãa* are not humans. This is where it can get sensitive and people would prefer to believe there's no debate here. I'm either lying, or a racist. They just dismiss me for any number of personal reasons. I'm very pleased to know researchers like Ted Gibson and Steve Piantadosi aren't going to believe my arguments just because I say it. But they think it's worth looking at. They're undertaking this long research project that's finally coming to fruition with a paper that should be published in the next couple of months.

For somebody like myself, I find it very difficult to understand how you can be accused of being racist simply for proposing an idea about linguistics that may be radical and contrary to mainstream thinking. How is that racist?

Well, it can be interpreted that I'm saying: *"The Pirahã language is somehow primitive because it lacks recursion."* Of course, I'm not saying that it's primitive. I'm saying, through structural values, they've determined to structure their language in this particular way—and it's a fairly sophisticated way of structuring your language. I'm not saying the language is primitive or that they're cognitively deficient in any way. People just have this knee-jerk reaction, that if the sentences of the language are simpler the people must be stupider. But that doesn't follow at all.

Considering Noam Chomsky is a professor at *MIT* and clearly your most staunch critic, it's ironic that the *MIT* researchers you've mentioned are helping, or looking to prove that your claims may be valid. It's entirely possible that they will find recursion may not actually be the foundation of universal grammar.

Well, they're not in the same department as Chomsky. Chomsky is in linguistics and their primary base is in brain and cognitive sciences.

I believe the initial research that the researchers have done has been dismissed outright by Professor Chomsky. Now, you've got what I would assume to be a credible, clear document being published. So, is Professor Chomsky dismissing this research out of self-interest, or do you think there might be a credible reason for his skepticism?

Chomsky has made a statement and he believes that language is this way. Perhaps in his mind, if I'm saying that it's not actually this way, I can't possibly know what I'm talking about. Chomsky doesn't believe that culture has any effect whatsoever on grammar—as he defines grammar. He doesn't believe that there can be a language like the one I'm describing, even though he's never done field research or anything remotely like field research. Chomsky has been through a lot of debates in the last 50 plus years, and he's won most of them. I don't think he's inclined to take critics particularly seriously. I've known Chomsky personally for over 28 years, not that well, but my office was very close to his at *MIT* when I was a visitor there and we talked frequently. He's very convinced that he's right and that's the main motivation.

Will the publication of this paper to change things for you?

I don't know what they're going to say in the paper. I have a sense of what they might say because they're using data that I know very well. The main thing is that people believe this is turning into a scientific debate and ceases to be name calling.

Whether Chomsky and his closest circle agrees or is convinced is hard to say, but it's unlikely that they would be. The interesting thing about the reactions from Chomsky's side is that when this first came out they said that I had to be lying. The next thing is they tried to say that I'm completely wrong, so they published articles criticizing me. The third thing they're saying is: *"He's right, but it's totally irrelevant."* Now there they are saying something new: *"Even though all languages are built on recursion there can be exceptions, so Pirahã is just an exception."*

But that doesn't really follow because, if you say: *"Every swan is white"* and then I present a black swan, that's not just an exception that's a counterexample. That means not every swan is white. They're trying to get away from the consequences of the clear claim that Chomsky made when they said: *"It's irrelevant."* They remove it from all empirical foundation.

One of your Brazilian linguist colleagues suggests that the reaction against your work will be described as: *"Science becoming religion, where believers will not listen to an alternative proposition and nothing can be questioned."* **This is ironic considering your own past with religion. How can you overcome this fervor for support of Chomsky's initial claim on universal grammar, because you must be acutely aware of the power of religious belief?**

Absolutely. The fervor comparisons with religion are, indeed, very strong. One of the reasons I've accepted so many invitations and traveled so much, when I would rather be home with my wife, is that by doing this, talking and answering questions from anybody—even the severest critics—people can start to take this work seriously. Not that they believe it, but they say: *"This is a scientific proposal. This isn't silly. We have to think about this."* It's irrelevant to me what they think of me as a person. But scientifically, it needs to be seen as an important lesson that this language brings for our understanding of what it means to be human. For people to ignore this is to pass up an opportunity to understand the world better.

Your work seems to go well beyond a self-interest because of its wider impact and potentially the benefit that science will gain from this new query, questioning, finding, and fact. It seems that your approach is far beyond your own interest.

Yeah. It was beyond my interest when I first wrote the paper. I found these things out and I could have written on any number of things. My view was: *"OK, I've been here long enough now. I need to set all of these things down that make Pirahã seem so different to me from other languages that I know of as a linguist."*

Scientifically, it needs to be seen as an important lesson that this language brings for our understanding of what it means to be human.

So I published that in the journal *Current Anthropology* and *The University of Chicago Press*—who operates the journal—determined that it was an interesting paper, so they issued a press release. All authors would like to think they could control interest in what they do, but nobody in fact does. You have no say over who's going to take up your story and talk about it. That there's been publicity about this issue is simply a reflection of the fact that some people think it's interesting. It has nothing to do with self promotion or anything like that.

According to Valmir Parintintin—the regional coordinator of the FUNAI agency, which is responsible for Brazil's indigenous tribes—one of the greatest threats to the *Pirahã* are the missionaries. How do you respond to this, considering you yourself arrived initially as a missionary?

He's right. I agree with him. But he's trying to say that I'm still a missionary, and he knows very well I'm not. One thing that the film couldn't bring out, for obvious reasons, is that Valmir told me on the side that if I would give him a brand new *Toyota* four-wheel-drive pickup, with a value of about US$75,000, he would let me go back into the area where the *Pirahã* live. But I'm not going to do that—even if I had the money. Still, I agree that missionaries can produce very negative effects.

Missionaries, especially those who are fundamentalist evangelical protestant, may be in a situation where they're giving medicine and keeping people alive, and nobody else is there. Alternatively, you can kick everybody out because you don't agree with them. But you have to make sure that you do a careful evaluation of what's left in its place, and make sure that the people's needs are being met. With respect to the *Pirahã*, the FUNAI, which Valmir is in charge of, doesn't have anything to do with their medical health. That's another government agency and they visit about every 30 days to perform checks on the health of the people. The agent visits and stays a couple of days, then leaves.

What Valmir has done, which you see in the film, in terms of bringing in generators, and building a school, etc, is of tremendously questionable value. There some shots of *Pirahã* children smiling at the end of the film—and they have cavities. *Pirahã* never had cavities before this. Some of the *Pirahã* men in the film have gained 15 to 20 pounds in weight since I last saw them because of FUNAI coming in.

These are health issues. And I'm happy to see a school—to a certain extent—although I had a school for a couple of years, and taught them in *Pirahã*. But they eventually decided this was not part of their culture, and they did not want to continue with it. It's really not my responsibility to make decisions for the Brazilian government, but I do get really concerned about what I see as exploitation, and the wrong kind of help.

It is interesting, though, because the *Pirahã* have successfully resisted outside influence for so long. Clearly, something must have shifted for them to accept outsiders—even FUNAI— bringing in these additional things to their way of life.

FUNAI was never interested in the *Pirahã* until I started gaining more attention. This is one of the bad effects of the publicity. I tried for years to get FUNAI to help the *Pirahã* medically, because I was doing what I could. But I wasn't able to stay there year round, and I would try to get the FUNAI to come in and give shots, vaccinations, and this sort of thing. But they never would, because they didn't speak the language.

Finally, just in the last few years, because they met me, and they saw me coming and going a lot to the *Pirahã*, the FUNAI decided to move in there. But they didn't ask the *Pirahã*: *"Can we come here?"* They just moved in, and they brought in all of this stuff. The *Pirahã* were not fully consulted. And if you stop and think about it, they couldn't have been consulted—because they don't speak Portuguese.

Yes, I was going to ask about that.

A few of the men can carry on very simple conversations, to the equivalent of me, for example, finding my way to the bathroom at the *Eiffel Tower* in France. I don't speak French, but I know enough so that I could probably find the toilet. FUNAI's involvement was not something the *Pirahã* were consulted on, and they don't have any way of knowing what the long term consequences of this could be. But I do think that this change has come, and it will produce more changes. There's no question now that the *Pirahã* have gone over a threshold—and there's no easy way back from it.

By the sounds of things, all this has impacted their culture. I picked up a particular from the film, which the *Pirahã* often say: *"I almost begin to want that,"* **which suggests they don't hold much value for material possessions. There has been, as you say, a threshold crossing where all of a sudden perhaps material possession, or practical tools and possessions, might actually now be accepted.**

Yes, and part of the issue is that the government comes in and gives them these things. Nobody has worked for it, or anything like that, they're just given all these things. They're given cookies, they're given white rice, they're given fishhooks.

The *Pirahã* don't need charity, they're not poor. People see the way they live, and if they don't have any kind of ethnographical, ethnological background, they think the *Pirahã* are poor people. But the concept of poverty did not even exist among the *Pirahã*. They had everything they needed, and they were extremely happy—and well off. With these things, which have now been given to them, has created addictions. And you can see it in North America, here in the United States, in particular. This is how we acted 100 years ago, and it produced a lot of very negative effects.

It's consistent with pretty much most indigenous cultures where—not just a 'white' or a colonization style impact on culture, but an outside influence—brings all of these supposed trinkets, and gifts. But they are loaded with an agenda, and introduced without any consideration. And the impact on that culture is irreversible. Is this something that you're seeing with FUNAI?

Yes, there's going to be a major shift in the history of the *Pirahã*.

That's sad. But I guess the alternative—as noble as it might sound—is to want the *Pirahã* to exist in a glass case, untouched, while the rest of the world changes. But is that irresponsible of us?

No, I don't say that. First of all, it really is their decision—not mine. Nobody has a crystal ball, I can't see how the decisions I make today are really going to work out in several years, and so I don't expect them to be able to do that, either. It's their decision, and every culture changes like this. I buy things from other countries. But my biggest concern is the way it's being done, and the way it's being done is to create a need for capitalist culture without teaching the people.

If you're going to give people this insatiable desire for capitalist goods, you've got to teach them a little bit about the other side of capitalism. If you don't earn these things, you're dependent on someone else to give them to you. This is the way it's being done. But again, it's easy for me to say this from the outside. I truly love the *Pirahã* and I trust their wisdom. They're going to do what they think is right, and it's their job to make that choice, not mine.

Speaking of other indigenous cultures, in Australian Aboriginal culture *land* and *place* are inseparably linked. In your opinion, is environment a key factor for indigenous languages, and can language actually be altered if the location changes? For example, an indigenous group moving to a town, or a city.

As I mentioned earlier, the *Pirahã* don't have numbers, they don't have ways of getting around, so within their environment everything is mapped out. If you suddenly take them out of that environment, for example to the city, where nothing is mapped out in their head, they're going to be totally lost for a while. They have to figure out how to navigate cognitively and physically, through a completely foreign environment. It would be like if you just took me out of Boston and dropped me in the middle of the Antarctic, I would be totally lost, I'd probably die before I found myself.

Plus, aside from physically and cognitively, they don't have the language to navigate that space, either.

Right, their language developed for a particular culture, and that culture developed for a particular place. If you move from the place, you change the cultural basis; you break the link between culture and place, and then you start to affect the link between language and culture, because now this language has to function in a very different environment, where the culture is no longer completely adequate, because they don't have these mental maps anymore.

Dr. Knut J. Olawsky is a German linguist working in Western Australia, specializing in language documentation, field linguistics, and endangered languages. According to him, he believes our language is defined by the environment we live in, including nature, culture, and social structures. He goes on to ask: *"How do we keep our culture alive if we don't have the words to describe it?"* **This seems to support what you are saying, particularly in the context of how the** *Pirahã* **language has evolved. It is tied in with the context of the environment, the nature where it is, and the social structures around it.**

I completely agree with that statement. My son—Caleb Everett, who is now an associate professor of anthropology at the *University of Miami*—has done a lot of work recently on the connection between altitude, and climate, and the languages that we speak. In fact, his work is getting a lot of attention, too.

And his research is something else that linguists have considered to be impossible. But he's done samples of hundreds of languages and shown there are direct correlations between altitude and climate, with just the consonants and vowels we use.

The first article he wrote has been reported on in lots of media. And he's got another article, a bigger one, coming out with a geographer, a professor and the medical school at the *University of Miami*, trying to explain the physiology and the relationship to climate, and how this affects the way we talk. This is something that linguists have also never thought to be a plausible possibility.

If we return to what you were saying earlier, about capitalism and how that might affect things, Dr. Olawsky also suggests our world is so clearly dominated by economy, wealth, and personal success, and that people are keen to acquire the language of the day, even at the cost of sacrificing their own language. Considering the *Pirahã* **culture, and their resistance to outside influences, how is it likely that they will adopt Portuguese, or another language in place of their own?**

Look at any language: Gaelic Irish, American Indian languages, etc. Languages tend to disappear because people exchange short term economic goals for long term cultural well being. We all do that. English is the trade language of the world right now, because of the economic power of the United States of

America, Australia, and the UK. But if China becomes much more powerful, if they ascend to that level of dominance, then it's very possible that Mandarin will become the most powerful language. People look for quality of life in the short term, and very few of us are able to think very intelligently about the long view.

Your estimation of the *Pirahã* population is around 700. My concern is that, with all this outside influence, along with the impact on their culture, it might begin to create divisions within the people, pull them away from their land and culture. The result would be a sudden decimation of the *Pirahã*. Would you agree?

Well they're basically very sturdy. The fact they're now getting regular vaccinations against all the outside diseases, which used to kill them, is a good thing. For example they are vaccinated against measles, and they also get treated when they get a common cold. A common cold for a *Pirahã* could be deadly. They also get treatment for infections and malaria, another big killer. Now that the government—not the FUNAI, but the health agency—is wiping these things out, the people are better off in terms of disease, though not necessarily in terms of cavities and being in physical shape, and that sort of thing. But they're generally doing better than ever.

Do you think that—because of the nature of their language and how it's linked with their surrounding environment and their culture, and in context of how they live—perhaps this might actually protect them. As you said earlier, to remove them from their specific environment to a new place, they'd be lost. Perhaps there language will protect them, encouraging them to stay where they are—and thrive where they are. Do you think that's possible?

It's possible. Their language is a very powerful cultural force, but you know, they're in a situation, as I've said, which they've never been in before. So it's really difficult to determine. Outsiders might visit. But, often what happens is they bring in a generator, and you film it while there. But then it runs out of fuel two days later, and they don't use it again for another seven months.

Due to this the effect is going to be mitigated tremendously. But to the degree that the government is visiting frequently, and doing things that are unlike *Pirahã* culture, and not really fitting with *Pirahã* values, the changes are going to be much more difficult to protect. And likely more profound.

I'll finish on, perhaps, a bigger question: Considering the environmental crisis we all face, many argue that it is in our own interest—and in the interest of every living plant and animal—to actively learn and implement aspects of indigenous cultures. For example, the *Pirahã* have no buildings. I realise this may have changed since the FUNAI have come in, but generally their culture is to have no buildings. They have no cultivation, or agriculture. They rely totally on nature, and live in complete unison with their surroundings. As you mentioned earlier, they know every species of flora and fauna that surrounds them, and they live entirely in the present—and they appear to be very happy about that fact. Is it realistic for modern society to incorporate some aspects of that way of life? Is it even practical?

It is, but you can't just do this in a superficial way. You have to really understand these cultures. If they disappear we lose the opportunity to understand them. But I would say the greatest lesson of the *Pirahã*, which can be easily learned, is self sufficiency. There are so many lessons. Every single language culture pairing on the face of the earth—and there are over 7,000—has learned to cope with the world and has been very effective. Otherwise, they would be dead. They've solved problems and come up with philosophies, and classifications of nature that are all of value. As these disappear, we lose opportunity to collect information that can be very important for our species. Information from each one of these pairings has taken centuries to develop, and they're a far greater resource for our survival as humans than any other thing in nature—I'm sure of it. We need to study them. We need to learn the lessons they have to teach us. And we have lessons for them, as well. We need to help them learn to navigate through these changes. It's a mutual relationship.

I did say I was going to finish on that question, but one last question has just come to mind. You're going to have a paper published. It's likely that paper will include evidence to support your claims about language, and recursion, and universal grammar. If all this is accepted, even by your

As these [languages] disappear, we lose the opportunity to collect information that can be very important for our species.

critics, you are possibly are on the cusp of changing our understanding of human language, forever. Are you prepared for that?

I'm prepared in the sense that, it's the *Pirahã's* language which would be affecting this. I'm just a reporter.

Though, I guess it's actually more than that. I had to figure out the language, and how it works, and this is difficult work. But there are hundreds of linguists studying other languages around the world, and those people are learning things of no less significance than the *Pirahã*. One of the problems with linguistic theories being done at large universities, and by people who don't do much field research, is that they get a very myopic view of what humans are like, and what languages are like. All these languages have profound things to teach us. They should all affect our understanding of human language. *Pirahã* is a very exciting case, because it has so many interesting things in that one language. But there are plenty of other languages, and lots of other linguists working just as hard as I ever did, to make these facts known. And we really need to know what those languages can teach us.

The writing on the wall: Notes from the field #5, London

An essay by Anne Miltenburg

We see G. standing in the middle of the bus lane, in an immaculate pin striped suite, and a light blue shirt (no tie), no jacket, no bag, and by the looks of it, not even a wallet. An Englishman who materialized, as if out of out of nowhere, as if beamed down on the southern axis of Amsterdam, between the carefully ambitious high-rise that is slowly pushing the Dutch urban landscape into the 21st century.

When he spots us coming towards him, he waves our car onto the bus lane and gets into the passenger seat. We continue our way without losing more than 30 seconds on the pickup. G.—an internationally operating brand consultant, on the move with only a blackberry and a visa card. His twenty years of experience in the business and a slight belly are his only baggage. The personification of the London Office. Our big brother coming over to take care of business. Me, the kid sister, in the backseat, with a winter coat, shawl, gloves, an extra pair of flat shoes, a laptop bag, lots of wires, snacks, notebooks, pens and paper, and a clunky coin filled wallet. Feeling powerfully over-packed and strangely inadequate by contrast.

I bend towards the front seat and raise my voice to make myself heard over the car engine. What were his thoughts on the creative work I had prepared for the meeting. *"Interesting."* G. replies, and after a short pause, he repeats himself: *"interesting."* Silence. Content with this positive note, I lean back and relax.

Looking back, I should have instantly known that this was not the complement I interpreted it to be. Continental Europeans often live under the false assumption that we speak English fluently, and understand it perfectly, based on the many hours spent during our lifetime watching [English soap opera] *Eastenders*, in the belief that this experience somehow adds up to a complete in-depth understanding of British culture. But Continentals hardly ever test their knowledge, and consequently, our illusions are left intact. In my case, until a shared project with G.

The start of our projects seems promising. During our presentation to the client that afternoon, G. shines like the consultant he struck me to be. We perform the *big brother / kid sister* act to perfection. G. racing through slides of lingo and 'bizz' speak, adding a little extra literary sensibility to his words, betraying a former high-school passion for Shakespearian drama.

One floor is occupied by the strategists, one by account management and one by the 'creatives.' Each floor has the props a film director would put in place to make the scene look credible.

Me, grasping for the proper English business vocabulary and combining it with an unwieldy Dutch tongue, but with just enough charm to be acceptable. On our way out, we exchange a handshake, and a quick *"sold it"* passes his lips before we go our separate ways.

For the next phase of the project, I visit G. on his home turf. From Amsterdam to London is a quick 45-minute flight: a take-off and landing without any straight bits in between. With the help of the one-hour time difference and a black cab, you can be in the office by 9am. On a chic street, a stones throw away from Trafalgar Square, a stately facade hides an office that reminds me of a doll house. Its main structure consists of several floors of open rooms, one after the other, in which various scenes of work are played out. One floor is occupied by the strategists, one by account management and one by the 'creatives.' Each floor has the props a film director would put in place to make the scene look credible. Charts and models on the strategists' walls, planning time-lines for account managers walls, and mood boards and wall paintings to give a proper creative feel for the designers.

I'm taken up to G's office and asked to wait. On the wall behind his desk hangs a drawing. It shows a home with a garden, and what appears to me as a 'grown-up,' 'a child' and 'a dog.' Above it, in the awkward hand-writing of a child: *"When is daddy coming home?"* G's assistant, a sweet looking girl in her early twenties, with long dark hair and a bright fuchsia angora sweater, catches me staring at it. *"Is this an ironic statement?"* I ask her. *"What do you mean?"* she replies. *"Did his son really draw this?"* I ask. The girl smiles and shrugs her shoulders, slightly shy and embarrassed as she blushes.

This uncomfortable exchange sets the mood for the day. G. and I struggle to get on the same page. At the end of the day, what could pass for a battle plan has emerged on paper. Just when I think—relieved—that we have a common goal, and I am in a rush out the door to catch a cab back to the airport, G. casually asks: *"It seems you are quite swamped, would you like us to pull the project to London?"*

Back in the office in Amsterdam, the ground is solid again. People say what they mean, and mean what they say. We also have our time-lines, creative work, and personal paraphernalia up on the walls. Unknown to our English colleagues, one of the more unassuming items on display is a list of expressions. It bears all the marks of being in heavy e-mail circulation, as the email addresses in the *fw's* and *Re:Re's* show. Someone in our office thought it was amusing and had casually put it on the wall—as a joke. But ever since I started working with G., I find myself seriously checking the list.

It goes something like this.

What the British say: *"Interesting"*
What the Dutch understand: *"They are impressed"*
What the British mean: *"I don't agree"*

What the British say: *"With the greatest respect"*
What the Dutch understand: *"He is listening to me"*
What the British mean: *"I think you are wrong (or a fool)"*

What the British say: *"I hear what you say"*
What the Dutch understand: *"He accepts my point of view"*
What the British mean: *"I disagree and do not want to discuss it any further"*

What the British say: *"That's not bad"*
What the Dutch understand: *"That's not good"*
What the British mean: *"That's good"*

What the British say: *"Please think about that some more"*
What the Dutch understand: *"It's a good idea, keep developing it"*
What the British mean: *"It's a bad idea: don't do it"*

Over the next few weeks, G. is kind and supportive on the phone—in a reserved manner, but encouraging enough for me. But after many late nights, wrong turns and dead-ends, I am loosing my patience with the cloud of confusion surrounding the project. And I notice I become guarded for those phrases which signal he is annoyed with me in return.

After confessing my unhappiness about our cooperation on the phone one day, G. tells me: *"I'm sure you'll get there eventually."* In a surprise move of extreme business saviness, he has turned my complaint about him into a pep-talk that suggests I'm the one that's not performing and in need of a confidence boost. I turn around on my office chair, to our list on the wall. I'm not surprised to find his closing comment there, literally. Underneath, it says: *"You don't stand a chance in hell."*

Gangnam Style: Notes from the field #4, Seoul

An essay by Anne Miltenburg.

"What is that word before the city name? Gang gang?" my mother asks over a distorted Skype line, while she is filling out an address label for a licorice filled envelope to my new address in Seoul. *"Kang-nam"* I shout, *"G-A-N-G-hyphen-N-A-M! It's the name of my neighborhood,"* I explain. *"It's so big over here that each neighborhood is a city on its own!"* My mother stares into the webcam incredulously, as if I was an arctic explorer who has just given a colony of penguins official land status. *"Never heard of it!"* she shouts back. And that's an end to that. Little do we both know that, in one year's time, there will be very few people left in the western world who haven't heard of *Gangnam*, the ritzy district in the south of Seoul, and that—when prompted—they will all do a cowboy-ish dance with a lasso arm manoeuvre.

The next day, I make my colleague G. laugh by re-enacting the Skype call with my mom. *"My mother better get used to writing those labels, 'cause I may not be able to go back!"* I say only half in jest, as we are sipping our lattes at a *Starbucks* around the corner from our studio, watching from behind the window how the office crowd hustles down the street. I have been in South Korea for three months, and the news poring in from back home fills me with a growing sense of dread. Tumbling banks, political polarization, social unrest, and a European currency on the brink of failure: it feels like I'm watching a fish caught on a hook, desperate spasms and useless twists. By contrast, my new temporary home seems blissfully free of these lines and hooks, and on a glorious path to world domination. *"Why would you want to go back?"* my colleague G. asks with a coy smile, tapping her hand encouragingly on her brand new, and very real, Chanel handbag. *"You could make a fortune out here!"*

As dusk falls, we make our way down to the subway station through the grid of skyscrapers, our path lit up by dozens of LED screens, like smart phones suspended in mid air caught in a perpetual loop of animated gifs. There's a business, shop or restaurant on every available square meter, and they all seem to take the power of illuminated signage very seriously. I have quickly fallen in love with Seoul's 24 hour economy, allowing me to play pool at four in the morning, or pick up my dry-cleaned suit at 7am, and with three dozen restaurants to choose from on my block alone, I have not had a home cooked meal since I arrived.

The 24 hour economy doesn't just facilitate office workers in their spare time; it has also created the 24 hour office job itself.

Nor had I thought of adding a Monday evening *k-pop* concert to my roster, but out of the blue, our boss insisted *G.* and I go—tonight! Record label *YG* was throwing a concert with all its biggest stars and the labels marketing manager, a business connection of his, had sent tickets over. Clearly, this was an opportunity to 'bond'. I hesitate. The Korean niche in pop music, dubbed *k-pop*, is a cultural phenomenon that I want to see with my own eyes, but there is a stack of other work to be done. The 24 hour economy doesn't just facilitate office workers in their spare time; it has also created the 24 hour office job itself. Noticing my reservations, the boss played the tourism card: *"This is something you have to see."*

I stumble to keep up with *G.*, who can reach speed walking pace on her 4inch stiletto's, even while balancing a piping hot coffee in one hand, laptop bag in another and handbag straddling her shoulder. Slightly out of breath, I suggest the Koreans should petition to add a *'K'* behind *BRIC*. *Brazil-India-China-Korea*. No change to the the sound; small change in spelling; but perhaps a big change in perception? However, once again, a coy smile appears. To *G's* mind—or so I make it out to be—Korea is already way beyond that coarse club of industrialist up-and-comers. I wonder what that makes me in her eyes; the old world European, hanging out with the *PIIGS*—Portugal, Ireland, Italy, Greece and Spain?

Down in the subway, the pulse of the city becomes tangible: a super clean high-tech subway cart with wi-fi connection arrives every few minutes, sucking the air out of the tube, forcing us to readjust our balance. A loud synthetic trumpet tune sounds through omnipresent speakers, as we board the Circle line in the direction of the entertainment district. The subway is crammed with hundreds of dressed-up teenagers with cat-ear head bands and giant bowties, confirming that we are indeed headed in the right direction.

As *G.* and I walk up the stadium steps into the darkness of the filled sports arena, I immediately get why a *k-pop* concert is every brand consultants wet dream. Tens of thousands of fans line the seats, their presence only visible by the glow in the dark wands with the logo of their favourite *YG* band.

The volume of screams is deafening. Video's on the wall of LED screens hugging the stage give me a crash course in the 8 acts we are about to see. The range of the artists strikes me as such a cunning balance of tastes that it can hardly be a coincidence. From boy-band heart throbs, to the tough-girl fashion forward band, to a piano playing ballad solo singer with long sleek curls: *YG* has all its bases covered. With razor sharp positioning, and an image honed to perfection, each act is a brand on its own. This is not just your average pop star with a line of merchandised lunchboxes. These are fully operating brand experiences. No wonder our boss wants us to chat up the label's manager.

The acts take the stage one after another in a carrousel of changing atmospheres, and team up in carefully orchestrated medleys; and up go the arms with the illuminated logo's. I squint into the stage lights, steadying my legs against the tremble caused by the ten thousand jumping fans, the hairs on my neck stand up straight for the next three hours.

The long evening provides ample opportunity to analyse *k-pop*. It strikes me as an amalgamation of western pop, hip-hop, techno, with a local language twist, but with more daring grooming and fashion choices. The short Korean syllables seem to be made for rapping chorus lines. The hardworking Korean ethos and discipline pays off in perfectly synchronized dance moves, and improved by an Asian aesthetic of dance moves, arm gestures, winks.

Looking at the artists, I feel a mixture of admiration and pity. The label controls all aspects of the acts careers, and some artists are scouted and enter training from as young as seven years old. Korean culture overall can easily be described as staggeringly ambitious, but the *k-pop* training goes beyond military style discipline: perfection is demanded in dancing and singing, styling and physique (with cosmetic surgery as a nifty extra tool)—far beyond what would be expected of a Western popstar. The acts sometimes have over 40 endorsement deals with product brands, selling everything from the coolest smartphones to ecological snail skin gel, or a new fruit promotion campaign by the South Korean government.

Acting talent is required, along with a good speaking voice, and a perfect face for high definition photo and video recording. The artists are trained in public speaking and foreign languages such as English, Japanese or Chinese, in order to conquer new markets. The Chinese music market will soon be the biggest in the world, and the Koreans have locked their eyes on this prize.

This is not just your average pop star with a line of merchandised lunchboxes. These are fully operating brand experiences.

One 12-man-strong boyband named *EXO* pursues the Chinese market rigorously, by operating in two teams: six guys in *EXO-M* (singing the repertoire in native mandarin) and six guys in *EXO-K* (singing in Korean). The world of business has taken note. One *k-pop* mastermind now even speaks at business seminars at *Stanford University*.

Music executives have discovered the soft power of *k-pop* as a kind of *cultural technology*. With catchy, easy-to-join dance moves as a virus, Korean pop culture can take over the world. But music is just the beginning of the *Hallyu* (wave) of Korean culture hitting the West. Cultural technology is an exquisite and complex ecosystem, recognized, understood and deployed by South Korea's government, industries and citizens, as *THE* method to build the brand of Korea as a leader in business, technology, creativity and design. And it is paying off. Korean children are outperforming their Western counterparts in almost all educational fields. The only topic that Western schoolchildren still outperform them in is, sadly enough, confidence.

Watching the perfect bodies on stage, with their perfect dance moves and enviable fashion sense, one cannot help but wonder if this highly competitive and ambitious culture is the reason behind the staggeringly high suicide rate among young adults. I ask G.—in a rather roundabout way—if Korea's military style discipline is not at risk of making robots out of them all. She shouts back: *"maybe, yes, uhh, maybe"*, and proceeds to wave her wand enthusiastically. The fact that entrepreneurs like Steve Jobs and Mark Zuckerberg dropped out of college and dabbled in hand-lettering is duly noted here. But military style implementation of serendipity and allowance of failure will be a more difficult type of cultural technology to implement.

When an older, rather average looking man with a slight belly enters the stage, the crowd goes wild. He's attached to a cable, and catapulted across the stage while making action hero moves, quite at odds with his physique. He does a lasso-throwing move and the stadium explodes. I don't get it. Being an outsider, with no previous exposure, I have no clue what the driving force is behind the particular popularity of one star over another. I ask G. who he is. *"He's PSY,"* she says, *"he's the biggest star of them all, he's really funny. He will conquer the world one day!"* I look at the guy again, and think: *"in the West, you won't stand a chance in hell."*

The community consequence of our creation

An essay by Andrew Barnum.

"To study the self is to forget the self." Dogen

"If your mind is empty, it's always ready for anything; it is open to everything. In the beginner's mind there are many possibilities; in the experts mind there are few." Shunryu Suzuki

We're all at a really inspiring moment of transition. As people, and as designers, we are being challenged to re-align ourselves, and our previous roles as commercial and creative crafts-people, regarding a more holistic outlook towards people, community, commerce and just plain old getting along with one another on our increasingly fragile planet. We are now at a point where we should investigate our actions to foster a rational and practical priority to work within the consequences of our crowded, electric re-evolution.

As practitioners within our commercial, craft-based tradition, conditions have now radically and permanently shifted. Close your 'chapter' dear friends, we're at a new starting point of opportunity—arguably as powerful as all the great industrial movements combined. Welcome to the 'post-typographic' age.[1] An age where previously ordered information—via typographic codes of agreed hierarchy, columns, grids and formatting—have received additions from new media formats, interfaces and 'motion interactivity' which propose new behaviours around engagement with text and image content.

Due to a re-configuration of the ways we now communicate, we are able to instantly connect with each other, anywhere, anytime. And this is old news. Any streaming media or world event, location, service, store, friends, family, contraband or even arch-enemy are now 'live' on your mobile device. This is a staggering sociological revolution, and in our suspended state of belief in the phenomena, we've accepted our dependency on this behaviour in the space of a relatively short timeframe.

While many of us have been distracted by this technological euphoria, there have been numerous developments. Shifting borders, behaviours, relationships and notions of experience have immeasurably 'changed' into something more chaotic and complex, and as a result, have sowed new social ecologies blooming with creative seeds. As a species, our *'adapt-o-meter'* is at full stretch. To cope with our steep curve of change, people

As a species, our 'adapt-o-meter' is at full stretch.

have quickly hatched ideas and prototypes, learned collaborative skills, prospered, failed and reinvented themselves in the fractious flow. Now, our collective challenge is to sustain this precarious re-evolution.

Our *'techno-pendence'* has prompted a re-definition of our interrelation with ourselves, and with others. We are all working within a collective re-birth of identity in these new conditions. No matter how secure you may feel in your current state of work and life, soon your situation will be shaken. And you will have no choice but to adapt and re-configure your outlook, your business-models, your experience of services and products and your newly public/social profile and subsequent online/offline behaviour.

Within the framework of 'enlightened self-interest', I'd like to consider how we might reimagine our creative practice for ourselves, our colleagues and patrons, and above all, the newly crowned *'User'*—that ubiquitous 'tester' of our professional processing, crafting and imagining.

This User is you. Not a separate group or sub-genre. You are part target audience, and part mirror of our own adaptation to change. You, the User, now glides within the networked world at will and with caprice. Previous behavioural borders of are now conceptually dissolving to be more loosely re-constituted spaces, archetypes, stereotypes, clichés, genders, nationalities, prejudices and motivations. Our experience is now a mash-up of inputs and outputs. As a networked citizen User, we are in a wide arc of discovery *together*. This fact will certainly influence how we now approach our practice.

With the sheer volume of 'creative' production appearing across networks, we have a new responsibility as producers, that will in-time, necessarily transcend our self-interest as practitioners. As so-called 'professionals', we will all need to help co-create our future through inclusion, innovation and a commitment to social-based problem solving. All the previous stereotypes of the designer will be archived: aesthete, rock-star, masturbator, geek, earth-mother, yuppy, no-talent wannabee, slacker, stoner, nerd, gun—you name it.

All these distinctions will be summed up by a ubiquitous persona, 'the problem solver', and this will be in the context of real-world

As so-called 'professionals', we will all need to help co-create our future through inclusion, innovation and a commitment to social-based problem solving.

conditions. Someone with a sense of humanity and duty, who puts their work ahead of personal award and rank within the world of design. An agent in service of the world and its pressing consequences. I believe the marketplace for design will no longer provide livelihood for someone harbouring previous 'self-generated' stereotypes.

This is just a hunch, but I believe the world is tiring of all the 'shiny design-talk.' Ask *YouTube* icon Reggie Watts. A mainstay of his music-led comedy schtick is the lampooning of the 'importance' of design: *'We talk about design often, at some point during every human's lifetime they will use the word design, and that's a big deal.'* [2]

Despite changing tides, we *will* rise to the challenges ahead. We are adaptable, tenacious and not without competitive vanity. We've worked through a remarkable program of technology-based responsive change from the late 1970s to today. We have digested a steady diet of compressed technological innovation and it's behavioural consequences as preparation for the connected, creative age that is now upon us. Here's a reminder of a few of our leaps ahead:

- Communication Technology: analog print and paper to digital and screen;
- Democratisation of skills from a pro-production chain to individual as author;
- Personal tech use: Walkman, Home Video, Cable TV, Fax, PC, Games, Mobile phone;
- Streaming digital media in cultural and creative industries, and immediate news;
- Web sites as commercial, retail, community, government services;
- Social-Community judgement of brand value and authenticity;
- Acceptance of Online Education as credible mainstream mode of course delivery;
- The rise of DIY Indie-culture as a tribal component of the traditional mainstream;

There are many more innovations that have arisen from the past forty years. Today, the potentially lasting changes seem to have stemmed from the following 'ideas' and tribes:

The sheer speed and uptake of these 'social modifiers' (see chart opposite) has been rapacious, and there is little evidence of any slow-down or disaffection. The conditions created by the combination of these 'theories' have created exciting and unpredictable times for 'creatives' and everybody else. We, as a world, have re-inhabited our ourselves as digital citizens, whether we are young or old. We should now ask ourselves how we as practitioners are 'growing out' of the previous and existing models of 'commercial service' between designers, clients, audiences and products. How we are adapting to the conditions of our changing consequence, and what is our renewed *collective purpose* of our creative exchange and intention?

With the explosion and democratisation of media channels and producers, independent editors and authors have spawned a generation of 'creative collectives' that are not bound by institutional methods or traditions. They create expressions of their spirit and have injected their communal aesthetic into the veins of the orthodox brand world. These 'wild people' have tools, strategy and purpose and have no connection or intention of extending any previous industrial tradition. Their software or authoring programs take care of that. Their key focus is on strategy, fun and truthful, authentic, emotional reaction by their audiences and peers. They are proudly outside the lines, prospering by ignoring any previous rules.

So, as practitioners of our great industrialised tradition, we are increasingly pushing a slightly mawkish barrow in pursuit of a tradition that's had its previous power and currency usurped. The new tribes are effectively re-tooling the creative mainstream, and its audiences are gratefully following.

I believe there is a deep-rooted philosophy at work here that has some of its roots in Seattles' post-punk 'grunge' movement of the late 1980s. An independent spirit with an appreciation (and distrust) of commercial constrictions and possibilities, but still deeply committed to the scruffy shared authorship that defined its arrival. The legacy of this movement expresses a mindful motivation that is moving our creative practice from one of creating materials or experiences that promote 'desire' for fairly 'mindless' consumables or services, to employing our skills, tools and discipline in the service of the *community consequence* of our creation. This collective tension between desire, achievable self-celebrity and responsibility, is both a hallmark and a shadow within the connected age.

THE CREATIVE INDUSTRY

'Convergence of Creative Arts (individual talent) with Cultural Industries (mass scale), in the context of New Media, within a knowledge economy, for newly interactive citizen-consumers.'

(Hartley 2005, p.5)

THE CREATIVE CLASS

'A class of workers whose job is to create meaningful new forms, new ideas, new technology and/or creative content.'

(Florida, 2002, p.8)

SOCIAL MEDIA

'Substantial and pervasive changes to communication between organisations, communities, and individuals.'

Kietzmann, Hermkens 2011, p.241-251

DESIGN THINKING

'Ability to combine empathy for the context of a problem, creativity in the generation of insights and solutions, and rationality to analyze and fit solutions to the problem.'

Wikipedia

CREATIVE ENLIGHTENED SELF-INTEREST GAME-CHANGERS

Today, any 'self-enlightened' practitioner should be re-considering the consequences of desire for individual luxury in an age with burgeoning poverty, hunger and homelessness, family schism and the general splintering of our social construction. In concert with remarkable social achievements across nations (eg. *The Arab Spring*), the connected age has also bred an underbelly of man's darkest intention (eg. *Boston Marathon Bombing*). Again, the world is a denser, more 'frictional' place to exist in, and we need to be more mindful of our production.

Today, our message-authoring has far more to balance in order to maintain relevance within the new experience of inter-connectedness. We are more than ever a shared humanity of people of every class and living condition. We are now more grounded by the spinning world of consequence and adaptation. We are more international, experiential and spatial, physical and interactive. We've very quickly evolved (or is it *de-volved*) from our previously reflective, ruminative and predictable consumption and expectation to something more immediate and vital.

It now seems plain and simple that our 'enlightened self-interest' should 'pivot' (this eras key descriptor of urgent adapting) towards a more User-centric, selfless purpose. From my foggy memory, the lights came on for me when I encountered my first graphic design mentor an eon ago. In my first job as a junior art-director in a multi-national advertising agency, it was made clear that the graphic designer had the power and responsibility to achieve more altruistic and aspirational goals towards the production of meaning vs. 'selling.' And for me, in our new conditions, this is more relevant than ever.

A more self-less attitude as a design professional seems to now fit the expectation of the network User. With the rise of the Creative Industry as a recognisable community, there has been a lot of 'creative for creatives' work produced of late. Designers are not artists, even though their practice contains artistry. Design is creativity in service of 'the design problem', art is deeply individual and personal expression. Sure design and art are in constant conversation, but their outputs are widely different. *"Being a famous designer is like being a famous dentist"* (Noreen Morioka from Adams Morioka). [3]

Today, what seems to be required to generate a livelihood is a return to adopting the persona of the invisible designer and

Today, any 'self-enlightened' practitioner should be re-considering the consequences of desire for individual luxury in an age with burgeoning poverty, hunger and homelessness.

his/her 'collective' of creative resource. The Industrial Design based, social design heavyweights *IDEO* personify the shift we're identifying. An on-call network: individuals, teams, specialists, collaborators, friends and associates who subscribe to the *heartfelt pursuit of meaning* as personal and commercial navigation for the times at hand.

Let's pause our reflection with a graphic that suggest the areas of discovery and focus to consider on the way to sustaining our more selfless headway. The over-arching ideas for the days ahead revolve around a more 'collective' sense of learning and realisation regarding the rising temper of our networked age within a crowding population. The emphasis for a constructive future now seems to lie within an adaptive, expanded approach to learning. Within our connected context there are undoubtedly more opportunities for learning appearing across communities, territories, sites, and by individual access. With our renewed 'explorer attitude' comes a critical need for a socially tuned approach to your personal curation of the tumult of mediated stimuli. Only by working together will we learn to shape, and form this collective future.

"If we look inside ourselves we see problems, if we look outside we see things to do" Zen proverb.

References:

1. *Post-typographic' age:* http://trove.nla.gov.au/work/153132587?q&versionId=166887417

2. *Reggie Watts*: http://www.youtube.com/watch?v=qDJZHWI894Q&list=TLO9bdJCs9beg

3. *Noreen Morioka:* http://thesherwoodgroup.com/interviews/noreen-morioka/#.Ugl3iGQpaLs

Expanding and including the **VOICE OF WOMEN DESIGNERS**	Identifying industrial strength **NETWORKING SKILLS AND ATTRIBUTES**	Course advisory membership of **D I Y DIGITAL NATIVES**
Promoting the collegial pathway to **BECOMING YOUR OWN PERSON**	Collective learning and instruction on **ADAPTING TO CHANGE**	Networked practice requires responsive **CULTURES OF THINKING**
School & University	College access to **PERSONAL CREATIVE MENTORSHIP**	Networked practice requires a responsive **EXPECTATION OF INNOVATION**	Generating and relaxing in remote locations **COLLECTIVE LEARNING PROGRAMS**

CREATIVE ENLIGHTENED SELF-INTEREST LEARNING PROGRAM

All our actions are interactions

An essay by Stephanie Akkaoui Hughes

All our actions...

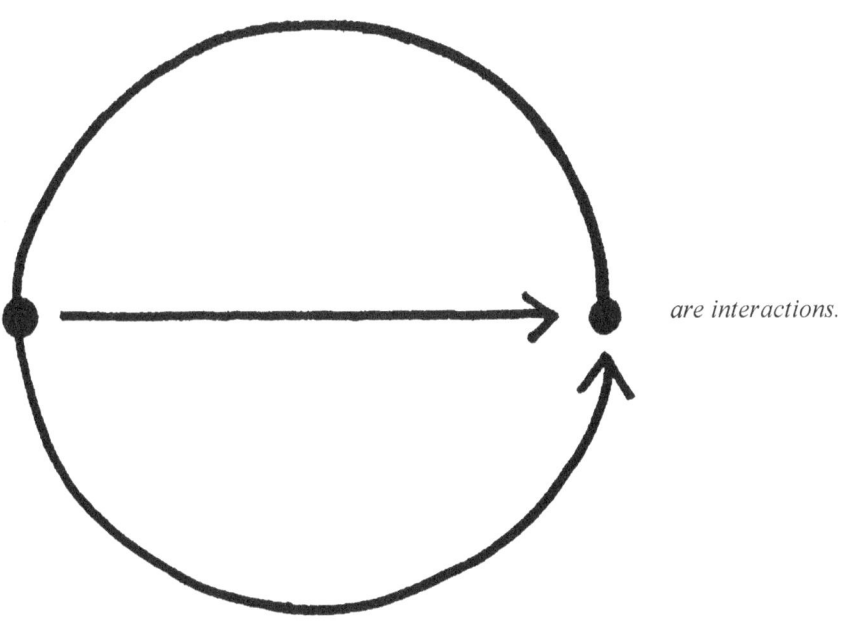

are interactions.

In today's world, we do not exist in isolation. Not only are we highly interconnected, we are also deeply interdependent, which means that my (well) being is dependent on yours, whoever and wherever you or I may be.

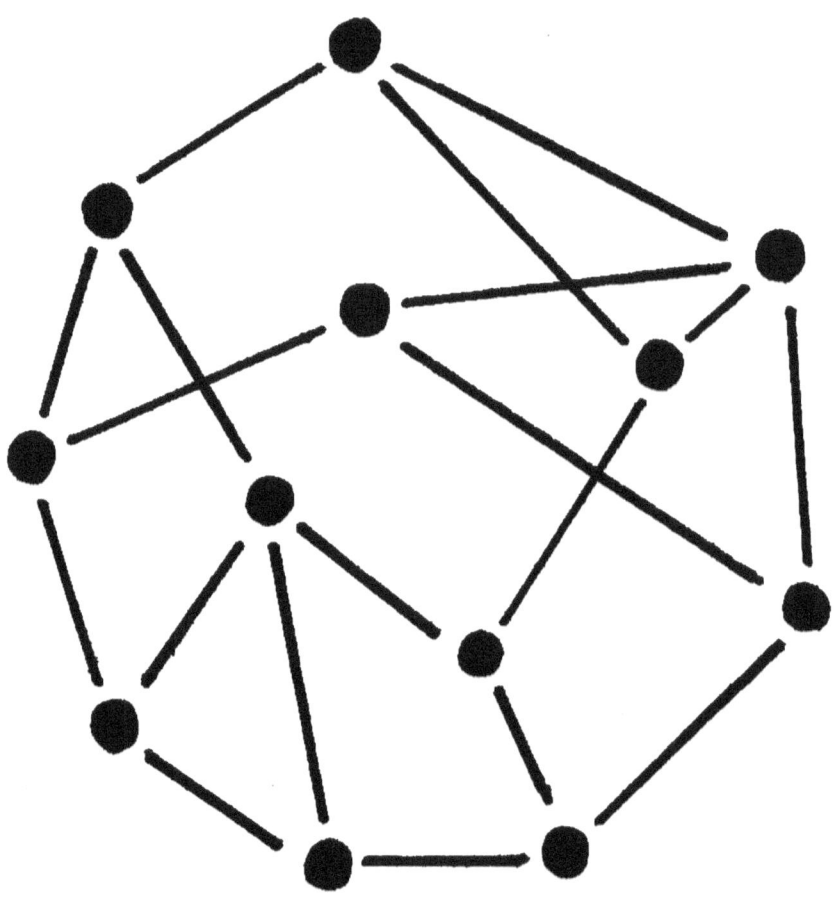

"The misconception that has haunted philosophic literature for centuries, is the notion of 'independent existence.' There is no such mode of existence; every entity is to be understood in terms of the way it is interwoven with the rest of the universe." – Alfred Whitehead

That we are interconnected is a fact, and our choice in the matter is limited; we can basically ignore it or embrace it. However, being interconnected carries a responsibility—and it demands that we act upon. There is no choice in this matter. If your being depends on my actions, then I am responsible for those actions and their consequences, beyond myself.

In the last century, we have in most parts of the world, looked at things in an increasingly isolated way, behaved in an increasingly solitary manner and designed increasingly specific, particular and exclusive solutions. I believe that fragmentation is at the root of all our global problems today. Because we are intrinsically and fundamentally interdependent, fragmented thinking, fragmented behaviors and fragmented solutions are not only useless in the long-term, they are harmful.

"[Design Science is] the effective application of the principles of science to the conscious design of our total environment in order to help make the Earth's finite resources meet the needs of all humanity without disrupting the ecological processes of the planet."– Richard Buckminster Fuller

Beyond our technological advancements, it is clear that our digital communication, physical travels, economies, politics, natural resources, human resources and environmental issues are all interlinked. To tackle today's challenges, to create opportunities in today's climate, we need to shift from fragmented thinking to *Comprehensive Thinking*.

Comprehensive Thinking demands converging and collaborating towards a common goal in the *Global Interest*.

However, 'enlightened self-interest', the theme of this issue—and which is clearly an improvement over plain old self-interest—it is not enough anymore. It is 'too little, too late' at this stage. We have reached such a drastic situation that moving one step up from 'self-interest' to 'enlightened self-interest' is not enough. We need to step up to a third level. The goal of self-interest is clearly one's self. The goal of enlightened self-interest is indeed still one's self, only on the way to that goal, one benefits others. The third level we need to step up to now requires a change of goal. At this third and more mature level, the goal needs to be a *global* goal. Today we need not speak of enlightened self-interest but rather of *Global Interest. (Illustrated in the diagram overleaf.)*

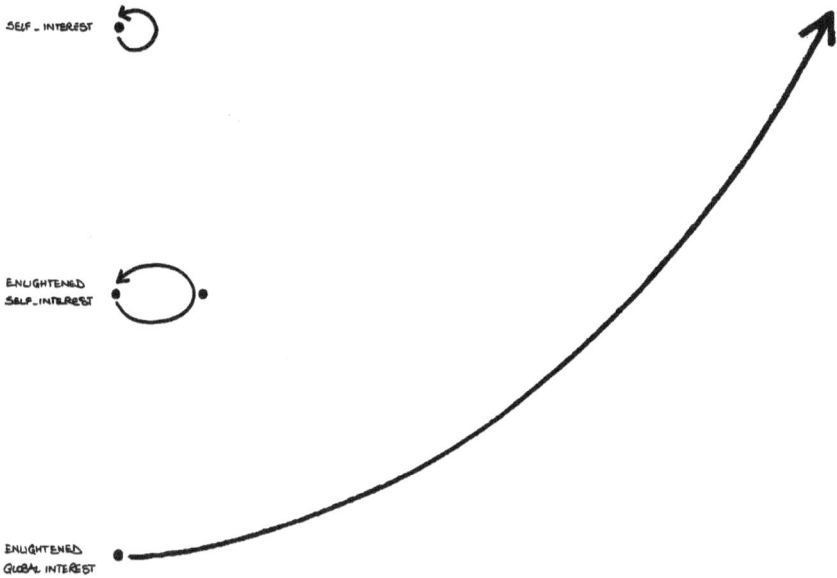

This might sound like an obvious shift. However, working towards 'Global Interest' assumes that we know what Global Interest is. Unfortunately, and generally speaking, it appears this is not the case. Although we can all intuitively sense the general direction, none of us actually know exactly what it entails. Since Global Interest is global (i.e. comprehensive), it is beyond the knowledge of any one individual.

To understand Global Interest comprehensively, we therefore need to understand its different facets. The closest way we have of achieving this comprehensive understanding is collaboration. A collaborative process, when done correctly, is an enlightened process. This is when we can speak of *'Enlightened Global Interest'*.

There is a reason why I refer to Global Interest as such, and not as 'Communal interest'. 'Communal' would refer to the common interest of a number of people, on a 'flat common plane'.

On the other hand 'global' introduces a larger dimension and puts the communal in relation—and in perspective—with the higher order of things, in an 'encompassing way'.

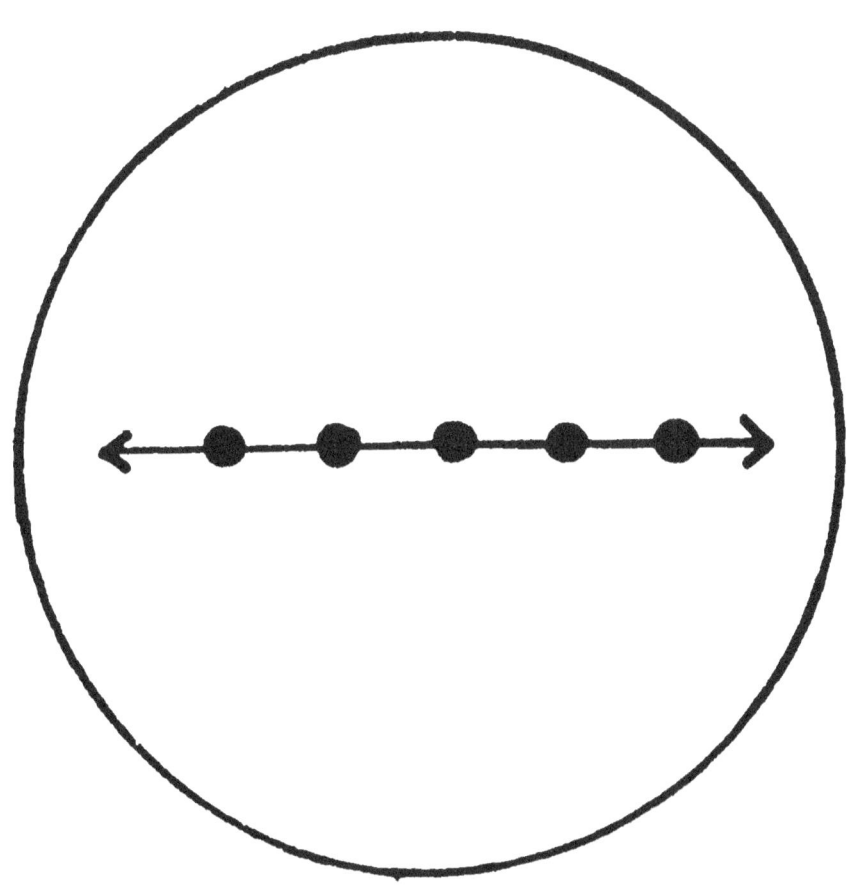

Global Interest includes the people and the land, urban or rural, the environment and Nature, for both the present and future. This is the real mission of sustainability; creating a situation that sustains itself over time.

On a very prestigious university campus, one of the buildings (which was one hundred and fifty years old) needed repair. This building was exquisitely beautiful, made of solid wood, with ceiling beams made of large whole oak tree trunks. These majestic oak beams were falling apart and needed replacement. To remedy the situation, the university faculty came together and consulted over a way to replace those large tree logs. Such oak logs were scarce and expensive and the department, not prepared for such events, did not have the budget needed. The only option they found themselves left with was to vacate the building and give it up.

One of the younger members of staff, not ready to give up yet, pleaded for more time. A couple of weeks later, she returned 'enlightened', and suggesting a solution. In her investigation, she discovered the architect who designed the building (a couple of centuries ago), had indeed predicted that the oak logs would need replacement around about this time and he had—back then—planted a small group of oak trees a few miles from the campus, with the specific purpose of replacing the ceiling beams of the building.[1]

Now this is sustainability in action; this is indeed Global Interest and proves sustainability is not a new concept but rather a very old practice.

I believe the underlying foundation of Global Interest is Comprehensive Thinking. Comprehensive Thinking means co-creating new alternatives to respond to today's local and global challenges. This is what I call 'Comprehensive Innovation'. Beyond the invention of new gadgets, products and services, Comprehensive Innovation means thinking anew and devising new solutions and—more importantly—new opportunities in today's climate.

I believe that the essence of Comprehensive Innovation is interaction; Comprehensive Innovation can never happen without human interaction. More specifically, Comprehensive Innovation is driven by three forms of interaction: Creativity, Collaboration, and Learning. It is at the intersection of these three forms of interaction that true innovation emerges.
(Illustrated in the diagram opposite.)

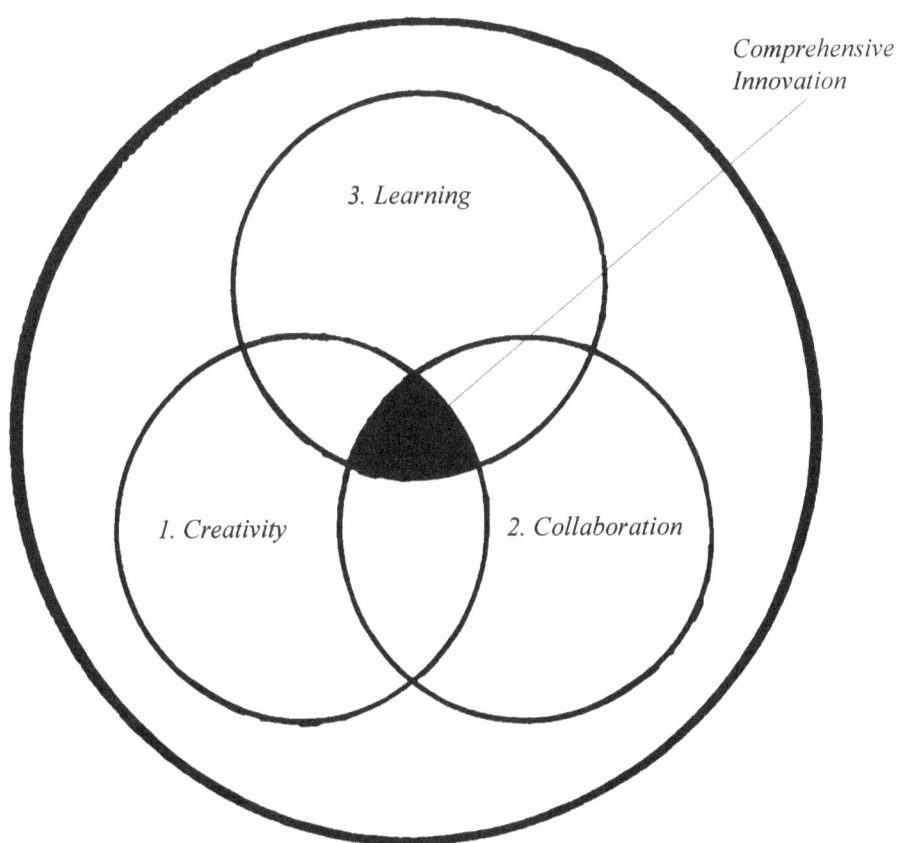

1. Creativity: the ability to create an idea, a product, a service or any entity that was not there before and that has positive added value.

2. Collaboration: the action of working together to create value. Fruitful collaboration has a time and a place, a structure and a process.

3. Learning: the ongoing acquisition of insights based on action and the ability to put those insights at the service of subsequent actions. This is *learning by doing*. It is a cycle of action, reflection and consultation that leads back to action. Learning by doing is intimately dependent on the skill one has to be sensitive to feedback.

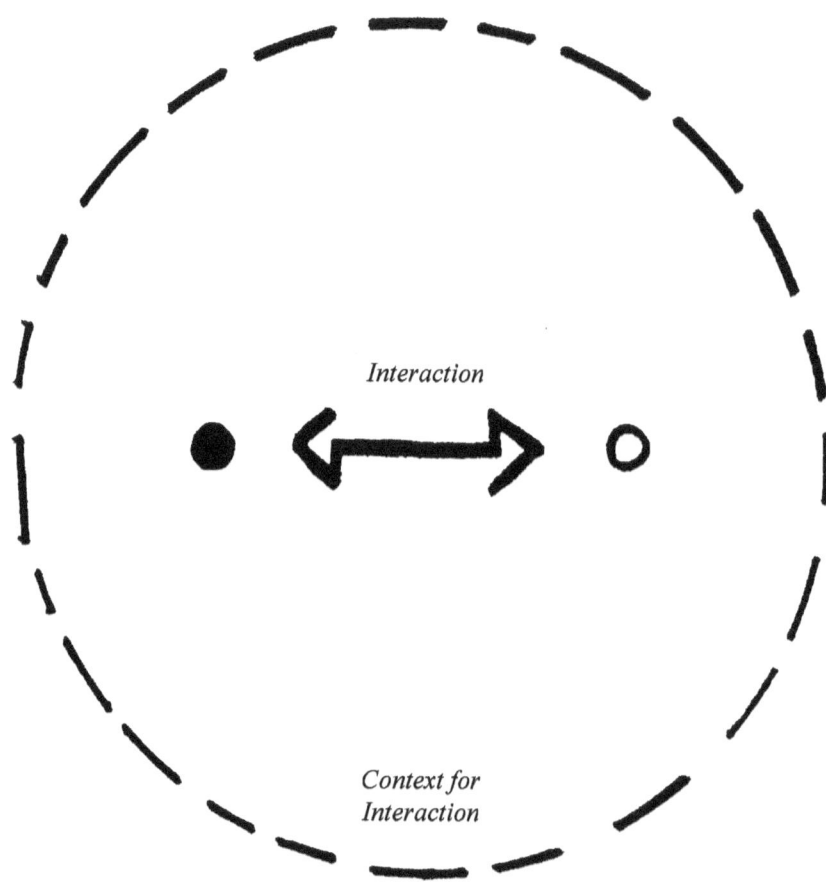

It is fundamental to acknowledge that we cannot design interaction itself; instead we need to design the context for interaction. In fact, we are responsible to design the context for interaction to emerge in. *(Illustrated in the diagram opposite.)*

'Context' here refers to the environment, the space we are in; and that includes the book you are reading now, the chair, the room, the building, the city and the people.

"In coming eras, the [human] environment will be conceived, designed, made and widely understood as a necessary part of our emotional and social life."– Christopher Alexander

So the question is:
How do we create contexts that trigger interaction?

I cannot stress enough that creating the context for interaction is everyone's responsibility. That is specifically—and literally—true for architects. As an architect myself, this responsibility has been a personal quest, and the source of *Architecting Interaction©*, which you might call my personal vision for architecture and design.

Through my practice I actively explore how we can design environments that foster human interaction. This exploration stretches on a scale of interventions; a scale ranging from products and furniture to interiors, buildings and urban projects. There are a number of examples illustrating how designers approach this philosophy. Here's one of my favorites;

An architect was asked to design a university campus. So she designs and builds the different department buildings on the site. Contrary to expectations she didn't design any routes or pathways between the buildings. Instead, she simply planted the whole site with grass. After the first semester, pathways formed in the grass. The architect then came back and simply paved them. Not only were the paths in unusual locations—which the architect could never have predicted—none of them were straight. The architect honored both of these features when she finally paved them.

There are three qualities I'd like to emphasize from this story: the three qualities of human context.

First: the context is incomplete.
The architect did not finish or seal the design. Instead she left it incomplete, unfinished. Incompleteness is the invitation to participate, contribute and co-create. Designing incompleteness invites interaction.

Second: the context is impermanent.
The architect didn't cover the site with asphalt, but grass, which is alive, organic and in continuous conversation with its context. Impermanence creates flexibility and allows entities to be regenerated—recreated by themselves or users—over time. Designing impermanence invites interaction.

Third: the context is imperfect.
The paths that appeared in the grass after the first semester were unusual, rather than being straight. Imperfection invites us to celebrate textures, scents and stories. It reveals the history and character of an entity. Designing imperfection invites interaction.

To enhance interaction; to create human contexts, the aim is for contexts to be incomplete, impermanent and imperfect. You can imagine how controversial such a statement might be, let alone the actual practice of such architecture.

I am repeatedly struck by how uncommon it is to challenge such assumptions and even more surprised by the continuous resistance I—and a few others—face when challenging any and all of them. When I first started formulating the vision of *Architecture Interaction*—and even with years of experience practicing architecture—the fact that I was 23, a woman (an Arab woman) and working in a predominantly male or male-like industry, did not help.

Incomplete, impermanent and imperfect contexts are indeed a challenge to our assumptions and our current way of practicing, commissioning and consuming architecture.

To trigger or enhance interactions, a context needs to be human. A human context is the minimum requirement if we are to work towards global interest.

Typically, architects design and build projects. They start from a given brief and end their involvement at the end of construction, right when the building is ready to be inhabited. The minute people move in the space, the architects have gone. However, I believe it is precisely when people move into the space that the building's life begins and that is when, as an architect, I want to be the most involved.

I believe that our responsibility as architects extends into the life of the building. It is our responsibility to accompany people as they settle in the space, now a living space. Architecture needs to extend into *Architecting*.

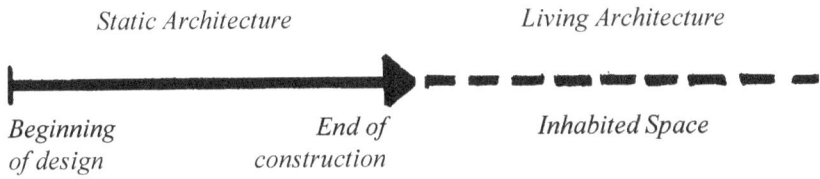

From the perspective of interaction: Architecture is static, *Architecting* is living. By this I mean, when we take interaction into consideration Architecture, as we know it, is a rather static practice and deals with the mass and the rigid. It is devoid of intentional attention or facilitation of flows and interactions. On the other hand, *Architecting* is living, since its very essence is designed around flow, movement and interaction. Extending the architect's involvement into the living phase of a context is crucial to refine the context for interaction. However, a simple extension of the process is not enough to create human contexts.

So the question remains: how do we create human contexts?

A vision needs an application. And in order to put that vision into practice, a process is needed. The following process is a fundamentally collaborative process, based on the communal creation of knowledge. It is a four-fold process strict in its principles, flexible in its application.

Understanding
'Understanding' is the first phase of the process. It is dedicated to (a) defining the *Community of the project**, and (b) using conversations to uncover the *Home Language*† of the project.

Community of the project: the people concerned with the project. This community is organized in concentric circles, starting at the heart with the people most directly concerned such as the users and growing outwardly towards less and less directly concerned people, such as visitors, neighbors ... etc.

† *Home Language*: a visual verbal picture capturing the essence of the unborn project, based on conversations with the community and the context of the project.

The foundation of this phase is indeed conversations. On the one hand, conversations need not be always verbal. By leaving the site incomplete, our campus architect started a non-verbal conversation with the campus' community. On the other hand, conversations need to go beyond people, and ought to include what the context itself has to say about the nascent project. Conversations aim at uncovering a shared understanding of what the project's own will is.

Envisioning
'Envisioning' is dedicated to creating a shared vision of the project's future with the project's community. This is where the Home Language is translated into a *Meta Plan**.

Meta Plan: is literally a 'master' plan, and not necessarily an urban plan, as used in the architectural world. The Meta Plan is the ultimate vision for what the project ought to become, highlighting its intention, outlines and large strokes.

The foundation of this phase is uncovering the project's shared vision, which is essential to create a truly human environment. Looking at the campus' story once again, the architect created the space for people to express their shared vision and the paths only emerged as a result of the community's accumulated collective contributions.

Creating
'Creating', the third phase of the process, is dedicated to making. This is where detailed design and implementation takes place. The foundation of this phase is 'learning by doing'; taking an action, reflecting on it, consulting about it and allowing it to inform the next action. These repetitive feedback loops help achieve a project better suited to the community. The campus' paths were only paved by the architect *after* the feedback of the community became clear.

Adapting
'Adapting' is the fourth phase of the process. Modern architecture might refer to it as the 'post-execution phase'. It is currently completely nonexistent, however I strongly believe it is an intimate part of the process.

This phase is dedicated to the final adjustments needed to make sure the project and the community are well adapted and living. This is what I call *Architecting*. The need for these adjustments can only become visible over time, and once the community is back in a normal mode of operation. The foundation of this phase is observation and sensitivity to feedback. One last time, we look at the campus' architect and learn from her way of observing the paths being created by the community, before adapting the final result to their feedback.

This process has an important prerequisite; it requires a fundamental shift of roles. The role of the architect has to shift from being a dictator to being a facilitator. We now have new roles. We now *have to have* new roles.

Architecture is a service. Assuming the role of a facilitator allows us to adopt a continuous posture of serving. This is the seed of what I like to think of as *Servant Architecture*.

The last phase of our process, Adapting, actually leads to a renewed understanding of our project's community, which means we are guided back into our first phase of Understanding. The process is not linear, but in fact circular. *(Illustrated in the diagram overleaf.)*

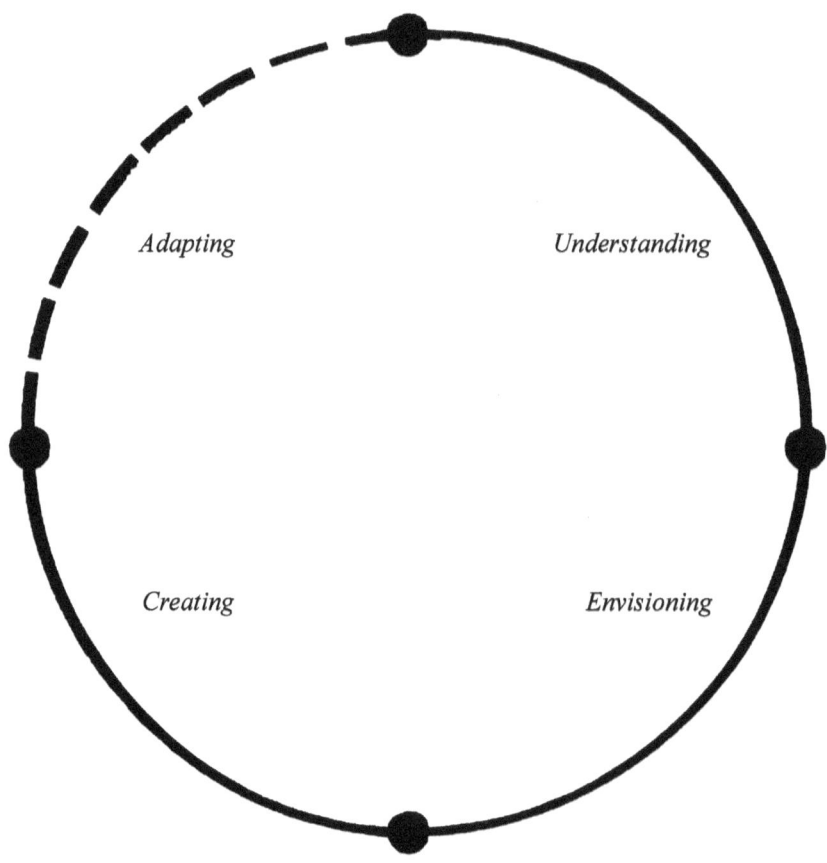

To go back to our question one last time: how can we create contexts for interaction?

This process illustrates how we can create contexts for interaction. This circular process is, in itself, the context where interaction will emerge.

Creating contexts for interaction, this is the essence of *Architecting Interaction*.

Because after all, all our actions are interactions.

Reference:
1. Gregory Bateson, *Mind And Nature: A Necessary Unit*, 1979.

No logos;
No straplines;
No slogans!
Just culture

Kevin Finn in conversation with Helen Palmer

Kevin Finn: Can you briefly define cultural tourism?

Helen Palmer: [Laughs] That's a challenge in itself—not to mention describing it "briefly." The way that we [*Creative Tourist*] look at cultural tourism; it's about positioning a destination off the back of its cultural offer. The importance is that people are making decisions to visit a destination, based on their perception of that place's cultural offer.

That's not to say that the rest of the destination offer isn't important as well. Of course, it is. But it's the culture that leads the decision-making. It's also fundamentally about increasing the number of visitors and increasing the visitors' spend—and about changing perceptions of your place. That's how we address cultural tourism.

There is a school of thought in academia, which focuses on engagement with local cultures, which is how they define cultural tourism in a very quick, brief way. That's important, too. But when you're working in the sector, it is ultimately about more visitors and visitor spend.

When we talk about the culture of a place—a destination—can it be manufactured, or is it important to start with the truth; something that's existing?

It has to be authentic. It has to be real, so that people's experiences match or exceed their expectations. If you try and manufacture something your visitors will see straight through it. It simply won't meet their expectations; they'll be disappointed, and they will tell more people.

It has to be rooted in the place, the culture of the place. The history of that place is really important, as well as whatever the contemporary offer is.

Lets say we're talking about a city—though it could be a place—it seems to me it's in their self-interest to foster cultural tourism: lifestyle and culture, but in economic terms, as you pointed out. How do you convince local government, or a city council, to embrace this in a holistic and a long-term way, because it does have to be holistic and long-term.

Yes, that's right. I'll give you an example of what happened in Manchester. We have a Chief Executive and a *Leader*. The Leader is an elected member, and the Chief Executive is a staff position and it's the most senior staff position in a local authority.

The Leader would describe himself as a cultural attender. The Chief Executive would describe himself as quite the opposite. What he has really grasped and understood, over the last 10 years—particularly, I'd say over the last six or seven years—is the role of culture in the perception of place, and how important that is in relation to all aspects of a city, whether that's about opportunities for local people, local residents or whether that's about people who are working in the city, but also about inward investment.

For lack of a better phrase there are soft elements which businesses look for in choosing places to invest in, and those elements are intangibles. They'll have a list of requirements or interests—for example access to a skilled workforce and good transport infrastructure, those kinds of things. But their perception of the place and its culture could be a defining factor for them in choosing to invest.

That could be influenced by what they are thinking with regards activities their family can do there—if their family moves there—right through to what their employees or people visiting them can do if they're based in that particular location.

It's quite interesting, when you see local authorities deciding on spec to build some kind of business park in the middle of nowhere. That approach is perceived as quite out-dated thinking now. Unless it's something where you might have a cluster of businesses already signed up to move in, that's a different matter. But building something on spec, when you're miles away from anything, that's quite difficult now.

That's culture, at its broadest sense, and it includes what we refer to as the *wrap-around*: the restaurants, the bars, the shopping, etc. All of those other aspects are just as important as whether they think there's a good concert hall or good galleries, or theaters, or whatever.

When dealing with councils, you have to constantly plug away at it. But we also took part in Simon Anholt's *City Brand Index*, which is an international research project. Cities are ranked based on six factors. They ask panels of people in different countries what their perceptions are of those places. It was really illuminating for senior people in Manchester because it gave them an opportunity to see how people perceive the city—including referencing other cities that are doing very well.

Actually, Australian cities did very well, as did Canadian cities. Obviously, a lot had to do with good weather, particularly in Australia—maybe not so much in Canada. Also, safety and a good place to live, a good place to raise children. All those sorts of things. There might be deep-rooted perceptions about the New World, as it were.

It's really interesting, when you talk to people about their different perceptions of places. That was a long-winded answer, so I don't know if I've answered the question...

You have! While you were talking, a thought occurred to me about the *City Brand Index*. I assume it's a really good tool when speaking with local governments and city councils in the event of any push-back around investing in cultural tourism. It proves you're not making it up, not trying to push an agenda. It states: *"Here's an opportunity, and it's in your interest to at least consider it."* **By the sounds of it, there is a lot of work around cultural tourism already happening, and which you can leverage. But are there many successful models out there? Or, is it at a stage where it's still developing?**

It's really funny. As I mentioned in my talk [at the *State Library of Queensland*, Brisbane], I have technically been doing cultural tourism for over 20 years. But it's only in the last few years that it has actually been called cultural tourism. I think major cities—like London, Paris, New York—are perceived as cultural destinations because of the wealth and breadth of their cultural assets. They get a lot of visitors off the back of their cultural heritage, in particular.

It doesn't necessarily mean that they're doing a good job on cultural tourism, but they are way ahead of the game, in terms of people's perceptions, the number of visits, and visitor spend. They are always going to do very well on that score.

For other places, it's been a bit of a wake-up call in recent years. Those of us who work 'with' the public sector, and those who work 'in' the public sector, will know that you go through trends,

Major cities—like London, Paris, New York—are perceived as cultural destinations because of the wealth and breadth of their cultural assets. They get a lot of visitors off the back of their cultural heritage, in particular.

the latest things people need to look at. We've gone through a long period of local engagement in the arts in the UK: local audience development, focusing on those immediate audiences. Particularly the museums and galleries world has been funded as such, those with box offices and a pressure to sell tickets. But there hasn't been a focus on how to generate visits from tourists. Historically, the two worlds haven't worked together very much, unless it's been around a major event, for example like a *Commonwealth Games*, or an *Olympics*. It tends to only happen at that level of major event—and quite often sporting events.

The cultural aspect gets tacked on, as was the case with *Cultureshock*, which is a cultural programme I worked on for Manchester's 2002 *Commonwealth Games*. Yorkshire had the *Grand Depart* for the cycling tour, which was a great success. Those types of occasions are almost forcing the two sectors to work together. But on a day-to-day basis, they don't have a lot to do with each other.

But because it's now a priority for the *Arts Council England* and *Visit England*, the cultural sector's had to wake up to this. In saying that, I'm not sure that the tourism sector has particularly woken up yet. There are public sector tourism agencies, but the commercial tourism sector doesn't see a lot of return.

I'm not talking about high volumes of people outside of capital cities. As you said, Kevin, it's a long-term approach. I'd like to think that Manchester's an exemplar case study with the work that we do with *Creative Tourist*. In many ways *Visit England* and *Visit Britain* have validated that. But we're just a few years ahead of the game. We've been doing work in that area, specifically with *Creative Tourist*, for about six or seven years now.

In terms of wider examples, I'm not sure that I would say that there are too many of them. I think I mentioned—it might have been in the Brisbane talk or the one that I did in Rockhampton—that there are other ways to approach it.

For example, the French city of Nantes is working with a performance-based organization. They've created these really quirky films to show Nantes in a very different way. They're actually embracing this and using it in the official tourism promotions. I think we'll see some more good examples in a few years time, when things have bedded in and more people are taking it forward by doing different things.

Of course, when you look internationally there are some interesting examples. But what often happens is that they're funded for a particular period of time. Then the funding runs out and you just watch them slide back, or people move on, or they focus on the next thing they need to get funding for.

That's the danger. People lose enthusiasm and move on to the next big thing. I do worry that might happen, because it does take a lot of commitment.

There may be another danger. I read in a recent report from *Deloitte* that they estimate the *Sydney Opera House* will be worth AUD$4.6 billion to the Australian economy over the next 40 years. That's taking into account everything from land value, ticket sales, right through to its contribution to the national identity. I'd argue that's...

I'd love to see that matrix of how they worked that out!

It was reported in the *Independent* and I think the newspaper was a bit suspicious of the report. But I'd argue that's cultural tourism at work, probably at its peak, because it's a large-scale example. However, in those large-scale examples, is there a danger that it could actually decrease investment in other avenues, simply because it's a big-ticket item? Is it possible for other cities and places, which don't have a high-profile landmark, to foster cultural tourism effectively?

The thing is cultural tourism is not about one venue. Yes, it might be the flagship, but it's actually about the rest of the city offer. Sydney has a wealth of quality cultural aspects, and not just buildings—whether that's festivals and events, as well as places like the *Carriage Works*, etc. It's important to remember this is not based around one specific venue or attraction.

Of course, you might use one venue as a hook but it's actually also about the content. There's also a difference between a first time visitor to Sydney: The *Sydney Opera House* will be on the list, and they tick it off. But it might simply be they stand outside and take a photograph—and not even go in and see anything.

The thing is cultural tourism is not about one venue. Yes, it might be the flagship, but it's actually about the rest of the city offer.

That comment was also mentioned in the article: a high percentage of tourists said the *Sydney Opera House* was in the top two or three things that they would want to visit and see. I guess my question uses Sydney as an example, but isn't there a danger for other places, too, where city leaders might say: *"Oh, we've got that covered because of our landmark building. So the cultural tourism thing? That box is ticked. We need to move onto something else"*? **In your experience, have you come across that kind of thinking where city leaders believe it is just a one-ticket item and then they're done, moving on to something else?**

We certainly went through a period in this country around about the millennium where major capital projects were funded in lots of places up and down the country. There was a sense of: *"All right, we've got our big flagship,"* Obviously, Gateshead has got *The Baltic*, *The Sage* and *The Angel of the North* by Antony Gormley. There are a lot of major, major, capital investments. But what's been really interesting, is that people have realized it's not necessarily enough on it's own—that they have to work in partnership. Partly this is a result of education about what tourism really means, that it's not just about buildings, per se. It's about content. As I've said in my talks, it's about getting under the skin of a destination. So, if you're a first time visitor, of course there will be certain things that you want to tick off and you say: *"Well, I've done that. I've seen that."* But it's actually about getting to know a place and feeling confident to step through the door of those flagships venues. It's also about seeing and doing things you possibly wouldn't have thought that you would do.

The smaller scale, intimate, experiences are often programmed specifically with the visitor in mind, but actually have a benefit for locals, as well. Policy makers need to be educated, particularly to avoid thinking it's about having one big shiny *thing*. The focus needs to be around what's going to keep people coming back? And that applies to locals, as well as visitors.

It's interesting: you frequently mention the notion of perception. When marketing cultural tourism in a city or a place, you're belief is: No logos; No strap lines; No slogans. It sounds like you're suspicious of branding programs. But perception and branding have a very close link. How important is branding in all of this? In your opinion, how can you brand a city or a place?

I am a consultant, so I'm dealing with this all the time. I work with lots of clients and creative design agencies to develop identities. I've spent over 20 years doing that. My point about destinations and branding is—and I don't know if it's the same in other places, but in the UK—in the '90s and naughties, we went through a period where local authorities, in particular, believed that the route forward was to create a new logo for their *place*. This is the misunderstanding between the local authority profile and the profile of the place—and getting mixed up between the two. They believed they just needed a strap line. Frankly, I believe towns and cities up and down the country were hoodwinked by a lot of design agencies who saw this as a market opportunity suggesting to everyone and anyone: *"Oh, you need a new identity."*

These design agencies would do a little bit of quasi-research to find out about the *essence* of the place. Then they'd come up with some naff logo and strap line. I could reel off numerous examples. We went through it for Manchester in the '90s and got really lambasted for it—and rightly so. I think pretty much every city and major town in the UK went through this process, and some are still doing it.

It's meaningless. Just because Leeds has a strap line that says, *"Leeds. Live it. Love it."* What does that mean? How is that relevant to a local resident or a visitor with the associated logo? Edinburgh had the *Incredinburgh* debacle resulting in the head of *Marketing Edinburgh* losing their job. You can see it's a bugbear of mine: *"Suffolk, a curious county,"* or *"the curious county."* I mean it's all nonsense.

That's my frustration. I had a long conversation with Peter Saville about this and he has always said that good places don't need strap lines. Places like Paris and London. It's also interesting when everybody refers to New York with the *I (heart) NY* logo. People have misunderstood what that was originally set out to do. The *I (heart)* model is now used for every place, including Manchester. It's seems like it's everywhere and for every city!

Of course *I (heart) NY* logo was really about getting local people to love their local city and collectively do something to change it because it had gone downhill—so far that locals were scared of going out at night. Never mind visitors weren't going to New

Frankly, I believe towns and cities up and down the country were hoodwinked by a lot of design agencies who saw this as a market opportunity suggesting to everyone and anyone: *"Oh, you need a new identity."*

York. That was a very, very different approach but it gets used as this example by everyone, and at will.

(In Open Manifesto #4) I spoke with Milton Glaser, who designed the *I (heart) NY* logo. And Paula Sheer from *Pentagram*, also did a review on the logo (in Open Manifesto #5). As you point out, the misconception is that the *I (heart) NY* logo was for Manhattan and New York City, but it was actually for New York State. It was designed for the tourism board—for the entire state—but it has since been co-opted by New York City. Actually probably co-opted by Manhattan, ever since it has been associated to NYC, as opposed to NY state. And it has been co-opted by cities around the world.

But the *I (heart) NY* logo really represents an attitude—a lived statement. It's an invitation to adopt a community feeling about a particular space or place. And the *I (heart) NY* attitude has become vernacular. In and of itself, it is, perhaps, a logo. Perhaps you could even call it a brand identity, but it is gone beyond that because it is more about a universal feeling and an emotion. That's how I interpret what you're saying, in terms of 'no logos and no slogans.' It doesn't necessarily have to be a manufactured stamp.

Yeah, it's that challenge where you're trying to encapsulate the essence of a place in a single strap line because it's never going to be fully representative. It's always then going to be the result of generalisations. Actually, if you use it on another city, or town, or place, it probably would apply just as well. Slogans don't have that unique aspect to them. We've just ended up with lots and lots of naff statements that are associated with towns and cities.

But you also get it with rural counties. And it's a lazy way of looking at cultural tourism or place marketing. I think it's an old fashioned approach and it indicates people don't fully understand how to market places or how to go about commissioning it. That just disappoints me, really.

Does this apply to Manchester, because I believe Peter Saville, who is the Creative Director of the *City of Manchester,* has created an *M* icon? There's no strap line, but there is an icon. Is there merit in having some kind of go-to mark?

It's really interesting. I've worked with Peter for a number of years and he never wanted to have any kind of simple icon mark. I think in the end there was a bit of pressure on him to create something. He came up with the *M* icon, but it was never meant to be used as a logo. It was meant for specific uses, particularly when Manchester is doing work internationally and when you've got a lot of partners working on an initiative. In this context, it's a symbol of a unified city region, not just the city of Manchester, but the 10 boroughs.

For example, when Manchester goes to the property event held in Cannes, the *M* icon is used. Of course, there have been cases where the council has occasionally used it completely inappropriately, sticking it on job ads and things like that because, fundamentally, they're misunderstanding what it was intended to do. But generally, it's used quite sparingly.

Another example: when we had the *Conservative Party Conference* in Manchester the *M* icon was used as part of the welcome messaging around the city because, again, it's a partnership of agencies working together and to be there as the host city for things like those major conferences.

So in terms of marketing a destination, let's assume there is limited or no use of a specific icon, and definitely no strap lines or positioning lines. How would you then market that place? Is it through various communication channels that are specific and targeted? Is it through media, or what other people are talking about? Or is it testimonials from people who've visited? How do you market that?

It's sort of all of this. The interesting thing is that a blanket message across different markets doesn't work. Of course, it's the same for any product or service you're promoting. You do have to think about tailoring the message according to the market. When approaching this for Manchester, yes, we've set up *Creative Tourist*, which has its own identity. But we don't just promote Manchester through that vehicle. We promote the north of England's cultural offer. We never wanted to be wedded to, or to just be seen as, an official channel for Manchester. We've always wanted to be seen as being independent, which we are now.

We use lots of different channels, not just our own. PR is really important. The way you talk about the place is really significant

and, through the cultural narrative, how you articulate both the heritage of a place, through to the more contemporary feel of the place, is incredibly important. We have worked really hard on this. When we do campaign activity, for example *Manchester Weekender*, those strong heritage roots come through.
We don't shy away from our heritage as I think a lot of post-industrial cities in the U.K. do, trying to reinvent themselves as shiny, new, contemporary places. There's almost an embarrassment about our industrial heritage, but actually that's what makes us particularly unique and it's important because that's what we're known for internationally, as well.

We do a lot of work on the PR side but also in the campaign activity and how we draw through the content and use that content in lots of different ways. Adding to this, we have quite a contemporary look to the *Creative Tourist* identity. We use a lot of illustration to ensure we are not bound by photographs... Because what often happens with place marketing campaigns is there's an over-reliance on pictures of buildings, or people having a good time.

[Laughing] Yeah, *happy people* **stock shots...**

Exactly! They could be any city or any place. So we try to take a different approach with the quality of the content, but also with the quality of imagery—and all of that does come through, hopefully helping people identify with it more and in a way they hadn't expected.

I believe a lot of tourism agencies over the last 20 years when talking about particular destinations all ended up sounding the same. If it was a city, they all wanted to claim they had *this or that*: for example, we're near the countryside, or it's only an hour from the coast, etc. You just ended up with this amorphous description of places in the U.K. that could have been anywhere.

We try to bring more of the personality through; what makes the place different from other places. We do that with any destination, wherever we work, because every place is different. It's just, historically speaking, some places have lost their way in articulating what their cultural narrative is, or they're simply hanging on to something from the past, something nostalgic, a nod to their heyday—and they need to change.

You talk about *Manchester Weekender* and other events or initiatives that—if we take Manchester as an example—suggest the Manchester brand could be an amalgamation or an aggregation of various independent but connected brands in their own right, those you've leveraged and promoted collectively. In other words, it's tactical and market specific. So when a diverse range of brands are talking collectively about one destination, does that simply reflect diversity, because you're coming at it from whatever angle you need, and depending on the cultural tourism you're promoting? Is that where branding can come into play?

Yes. Also, as I said, Manchester is probably known for a handful of things internationally. One is football. One is, as we like to say, the birthplace of the Industrial Revolution. But that's always contested. [Laughter] And music, particularly *The Smiths* through to *Happy Mondays*. I'd say actually *Joy Division* through to *Happy Mondays*.

Now that doesn't represent the whole of the city, of course, but at least there is a level of international awareness regarding Manchester. And we have a job to do in changing peoples' perceptions, that the city is more than that. We don't have the flagship building that people will associate with the place, so people's visual perception is often really out of date because the thinking might be: *"Industrial revolution? There must be lots of factories and chimneys."*

Meaning: I don't want to go to Manchester because it'll be smoggy [laughs] or dull!

Once, on the train from Manchester to Stoke-on-Trent—world capital of ceramics, as they like to call it—I overheard an American guy talking openly.

The train goes through beautiful countryside and, although he was on own, he was chatting to anybody who'd listen. I won't try to do his accent, but he was like: *"Wow! This isn't at all what I thought it would be like. I thought there'd be lots of factories and chimneys."* And this is an educated man on business in the U.K. who still thought that 'up north' was just full of factories and chimneys!
Often, there are these huge out-of-date perceptions.

And we also struggle with the visual representation of Manchester. Liverpool doesn't have that because it has its waterfront. It has the *Three Graces*, which is quite an iconic image. It also has *The Beatles*, as well as football. I think a lot of places will struggle with visual representation.

I'm sure actually Brisbane has some similar issues, though it's quite a beautiful city. But I imagine people don't visually know what to expect because it's not known for having an iconic flagship like Sydney. That's always a challenge.

Now I've forgotten your original question as I've been wandering around with my response. Oh yeah! Brands—different brands! [Laughter.]

The way that we approach cultural tourism is: 'It's not democratic or diplomatic.' You don't always promote the same perceived lead brands. You promote what is appropriate for the different markets and depending on the time of year as well. Just because a major gallery exists it doesn't mean you will always lead with that as the story, because they might not have an exhibition that relates to the market we're looking at. It has to be market-focused.

The title of your talk in Brisbane had a rather provocative title: *Cultural Tourism: Curb Your Diplomacy.* **One would suspect promoting cultural tourism involves managing multiple stakeholders with multiple agendas. In your opinion is diplomacy in general, or in specific terms, actually counterproductive? Or are we talking about separate things...**

It's slightly provocative. Often, the way the public sector has worked in the past—when it's worked in collaboration—has been dominated by a perception that everybody has to be equal and that the profile, if they're working in a joint marketing way, everything has to be equal.

That's product-focused, not market-focused. That's very much about egos at the table saying: *"I need to get as much profile as them, and they shouldn't be getting more profile than me."* We just don't work that way. It's not about who's turn it is. It's simply about what's right for the market.

That is sometimes really difficult for people in the public sector to get their heads around, because they're fundamentally used to working primarily with the public sector. And the cultural sector is more often than not funded by the public sector.

It's not to say that there aren't private sector organizations that one might work with, particularly the tourism industry. Even so, it is still very difficult for some people to leave their egos at the door and sit in a room and think of the bigger picture. It's taken us a while to get to that point in Manchester.

I'm sure it's also influenced by those who say: *"Well, we've put this amount of money on the table, therefore we want to get this amount back."* **But the person with the biggest checkbook doesn't necessarily need to get the biggest megaphone.**

Exactly! Actually, on the whole tourism agencies are set up as membership organizations. So people buy into campaigns. If you buy into a campaign, then you get profile in that campaign. It's completely client-focused and not market-focused.

Incentivized for funding...

Campaigns help get information through but it's often on behalf of a random collection of organizations. I'm sure members of the public understand that, to a degree. But we don't operate that way. We're not a membership organization, so we don't have to include certain organizations.

We've historically worked with the *Manchester Museums and Galleries Consortium* which is not a membership organization, either. It's a collective of venues working together around different areas. They are big enough to say: *"Yep, fine, you get on with it. We know that it's for the benefit of the city and therefore it will benefit us."* But it's taken a long time to get to that point.

That actually goes to the heart of the theme for this issue of Open Manifesto: *Enlightened self-interest.* **Obviously, some organisations you mentioned have a self-interest, but it's enlightened enough to understand that it's also got to benefit other people, and the by-product will benefit that organisation anyway. The thinking is:** *"Because if it benefits everyone, it benefits us."* **We're talking about culture, but that must be a cultural shift for many organizations. Is this still a barrier for you?**

Yeah. Many of those organisations are publicly funded and the funding situation here [in the U.K.] for the arts is really difficult. There have been significant cuts, which have impacted on all the funders of the arts. And sponsorship outside London is difficult anyway.

The majority of private sponsorship and philanthropy that's going into the arts is in London. For some funders, if the *Arts Council* is seen to be behind something, they feel like they need to be at the table to demonstrate they're part of whatever the project is, which is not necessarily the right reasons for being at the table. There are also people at the table thinking: *"There's going to be money coming out of this. And I want a piece of that."* So it's vital to understand people's motivations regarding why they're at the table. In some cases the local authorities told them they should be there, or they feel they *need* to be there because of other people who are at the table. Then you end up with an unwieldy group of far too many people. And worse: whoever shouts loudest gets the attention.

All of them looking for an equal share of the pie regardless.

Or smaller organizations, thinking: *"It'll always be the bigger ones who get all the attention."* There's a lot of that to get through. We spend a lot of time managing those kinds of relationships and trying to encourage other destinations to think similarly.

Obviously, we're based in Manchester but, in the other destinations we work with it's about trying to encourage those lead organizations, which tend to be local authorities or tourism agencies, to take the lead because somebody has to take a lead when you're talking about cultural tourism.

The lead should be from within the cultural sector, but in some places it isn't. So it's about encouraging them to know how best to work in partnership and what the benefits are. If people step out along the way, then you have to just take that on board. We just need to accept that it simply may not be for them. The important thing is if there are big players in your destination, you absolutely need them around the table. There has to be an incentive for them to be around the table. And that isn't necessarily about money. It's an ongoing cultural shift where the larger organizations are encouraged by funders to think about how they support the smaller organizations.

There are also people at the table thinking: *"There's going to be money coming out of this. And I want a piece of that."* So it's vital to understand people's motivations regarding why they're at the table.

Of course, in the private sector it's really competitive but it's a very different experience when you get into the public sector... For example, I was at a hoteliers forum just after I got back from Australia. Now, I've been at different hoteliers forums in Manchester, but this one was for a particular part of the city, so not the whole city. Actually, because they were a particular area of the city, they did seem to be more willing to collaborate. But if you take a general hoteliers' forum, it's everybody in and everybody for themselves. I know this might be a sweeping generalization, but there's more of a sense of competition. There's a sharing of information up to a point, but then commercial sensitivities come into play.

Thankfully, many of those commercial organizations do now understand they need each other and they grasp the importance of critical mass. They also understand how things in the city are impacting them as an individual organization, as well as members of an industry sector. Even as commercial organizations they have to think in different ways and talk to people that they perhaps wouldn't have, even 10 years ago.

In terms of everything we've been talking about, does it matter whether we're talking about a city or a place? If you scale this up to a country—what we refer to as *nation branding*—**can cultural tourism in the way we're discussing be successful? For example, in the 1990s, you had** *Cool Britannia* **under Prime Minister Tony Blair's stewardship.**

I knew you were going to mention that.

Well, that's probably one of the more focused attempts at trying to create some kind of a destination brand around a country. Others have approached it differently, but *Cool Britannia* **is probably one of the most memorable, at least in my experience. Whether it's successful or unsuccessful in its objectives is a different question. But is it possible to scale these ideas up?**

What's interesting for me about *Cool Britannia* is that this was a national government attempt to reposition the country. And it's really interesting when you look at the cultural people who were involved with it in the early days—bands like *Blur* and *Oasis*. When it started off the perception was the government understood that it wasn't just about chocolate box heritage, that there was a contemporary culture being promoted around the world, particularly on the commercial music front.

But then they went too far with it and it just became naff. I bet all of those people who were originally associated with it now look back and cringe, thinking: *"I can't believe I was involved in that."* [Laughter] Because Tony Blair with an electric guitar is not the kind of image you want when trying to convey *Cool Britannia* around the world. It's just not authentic.

It comes back to the fact it's just a sound bite. It's that kind of politics that we had during that era, that it's more about the photo opportunity and the sound bite than the substance. It might have started off in the right place, but it really went in the wrong direction.

Visit Britain now has this *Great Britain* campaign, which they've been rolling out internationally. They're using a lot of celebrities to endorse it, including actors and musicians. But they're not necessarily people you would associate as being *cool*. They've got Stephen Fry, Julie Walters, Judi Dench and the stars from *Harry Potter* and *Downton Abbey*, among others. So they are internationally renowned cultural icons, if you like, who've come out of Britain and who are saying they like a particular part of the country. It's a much more mainstream approach.

I find when government bodies try to get across the intangible cultural *feel* of a nation, they will always slip back into generalities because it's quite difficult to articulate. The more you try to scale that up, the more general it becomes. I think that's why you end up with these very general campaigns that can often go off in the wrong direction.

I've been to events in Los Angeles, which have been organized by—I'd better be careful what I say here now—let's say 'national bodies.' The way that they've presented Britain is not necessarily the Britain that I know. It is hung on stereotypes. And that's not unique to just this country. That's every nation doing pro-active tourism work. They will tend to hang it on those visual icons: the *London bus*, the *Chelsea pensioner*, the *Beefeater*, those things that are instantly recognizable. But you end up with people thinking London is the U.K. You go to America and people ask:

I find when government bodies try to get across the intangible cultural *feel* of a nation, they will always slip back into generalities because it's quite difficult to articulate.

"Where are you from?"
"Manchester."
"Is that near London?"

[Laughing.]

The response I have in my head is often: *"Well, probably to you it is, but Manchester is a different world."*

What often happens is that those major capital cities tend to dominate the national perception and narrative about a place.

Yes, I think Australia has a big problem with that when it's speaking to the international market. It tends to trade off very, very clichéd stereotypes. It's a lazy way of approaching it because it could be done in a much more authentic, more educational, and more genuine way. That said, there are campaigns that have attempted to do that, particularly with regards to Indigenous culture. But it's sugar coated. It's stereotypical. The experience may align with a tourist or visitor's perception in the first couple of days but pretty quickly they're likely to see an entirely different story—which is the reality. Maybe that's the intention. Grab people in and when they're here, they'll figure it out for themselves. Perhaps there's room for an international dialogue, which isn't based on stereotypes or clichés. Have you seen anything like that?

What's interesting is that visitors are now becoming much more sophisticated. They are not relying on official channels or going into local travel agents and booking their holiday. My parents actually still do—bless them—because they don't have a computer. Well, actually they do have a computer, they just never switch it on.

The market has changed so dramatically that people will generate their own research about the place. And particularly in the cultural tourism world, the likelihood of them going down official channels has diminished—word of mouth is going to be important, but they also want to find out their own information. Of course, you can see the sales of guidebooks are plummeting. There's so much information on the Internet now that people will form their own opinion.

Now, whether it's right or wrong is a different issue. I mean, I still am amazed at how many people still use *TripAdvisor* when for me, it's not authentic anymore. It just simply isn't. I think in its early days it was a useful tool, but I wouldn't use it now. I just wouldn't believe anything on there.

Then there are a lot of people who will still listen to a stranger's opinion regarding a place and take their advice, rather than an official channel, which is quite an interesting shift. That's a massive cultural shift.

Take the stereotypes of Australia, as an example. A lot of people who visit will never go near the bush. They will go to the cities and the beaches. So there's a lot more that needs to be done in that dialogue. I think there's a safety mechanism with people hanging onto those stereotypes and those national icons, because they know it's a quick reference point. I think we're a long way from ditching that. The London bus example is really interesting, because the buses are completely different now.

Heatherwick redesigned them...

Yeah. So they don't look anything like the previous buses, but they're still the red bus.

A few years ago I spoke with branding guru Wally Olins [interviewed in Open Manifesto #5]. We talked about nation branding, and he had similar views to you, that it's perhaps difficult—or even contentious—to brand a nation, but the reality is that it will be branded through perception anyway. And when considering countries, they are going to be in constant flux, regardless. So his view was you're better off trying to at least manage that process, so that you can help guide the perception. There is a fine balance between branding—as we know it— and avoiding the approach of: *"Let's just leave it up to the people and see what they say."* **It's really about management. One of the principles that I use in my branding work is:** *branding is not what you say you are, it's what other people say you are. The challenge is managing the gap.*

Absolutely!

I believe this is what you're referring to, in terms of changing perceptions, but not using slogans. It's a tricky line to walk, but that's where it is. That's where it happens. It means you can be more flexible, though. You're not bound by one statement or one thought. You can move.

Exactly. Simon Anholt also does a *Nation Brand Index*, as well as a *City Brand Index*. There are certain groupings of cities that are based on perceptions of the nation, more than the city. African cities, Middle Eastern cities—they don't score well.

I guess that makes sense, considering the power of perception.

As I say, Australia and Canada score well. In terms of the U.K., the perception is that we're not very friendly, and that the weather's bad. It affects perceptions of individual cities, as well as it does the nation. There are things that are wrapped up with the national perceptions that impact on an individual place, and these perceptions are almost outside your control. But you just have to work with that.

That said, even though the U.K. is not known for its weather, we still get a lot of visitors, because of the quality of our tourism offer and our cultural offer. It's unique to us. There are things that you can work with and adapt to—but there are other things, like people's perceptions of the Middle East and Africa, that are generational and they're gong to take a lot longer to shift. And if a country is enduring political strife, that just reinforces people's perceptions.

Also, people's geography is often not very good. Africa just gets lumped in as this one *place*, rather than the reality of lots and lots of different countries, not to mention the differences between those countries. It's just a lazy way of thinking, but it also demonstrates people's general lack of knowledge.

You mentioned Peter Saville earlier. When I spoke with Peter a few years back [in Open Manifesto #4], one belief he mentioned about branding—and this goes to perception—is that, as a brand, it's important to be in the news. It's about being a news story, because that's going to shape more perception than any official brochure.

If we go back to the topic of PR, of media—but also if you look at those areas, geographically, which you've mentioned—when we see Africa in the news, it's usually not good news. When we see the Middle East in the news, it's usually either a bit awkward or not good news. That goes to people's perception of Dubai and Abu Dhabi and Tanzania, etc. Again, what Peter was advocating is developing your specific news story. That's where branding can happen, because that's where perceptions can get shaped or altered. It's not necessarily a traditional space that marketing and branding people will inhabit because, for a start, you can't manage it, and that's scary for them. But it also doesn't give them a physical output, a designed artefact—like a logo, or a brochure. Marketing and branding agencies still seem to be addicted to an output, rather than an effect.

Absolutely, yeah. The tourism industry, in particular, is still obsessed with leaflets and brochures. The Arts are too, to some extent, but the tourism industry in particular. It's as if when they wonder what they should do someone says: *"Let's produce a leaflet."* They're not market-focused, and they're scared of making dramatic changes. Their default position is: *"It's worked in the past, so we'll do that again."*

Most organizations are really well behind the curve when it comes to digital engagement. This is something we tackle quite a bit with *Creative Tourist*. That's one of our strengths. It can be quite frustrating when talking to other organizations, places, clients, whatever, when they're well behind on that journey.
The public sector is particularly well behind. Now, I'm not saying that the commercial tourism sector is necessarily at the forefront, but they've certainly understood the potential a lot quicker.

Many fall back to their safety net: *"We'll do what we've always done. And we need a website, as well. We have to be on social media, too."* But they say this without understanding what engagement with consumers is now about, or the importance of content-led marketing, because there isn't a physical output.

All bias aside, the fact Manchester now has two world-class football clubs, and the messages this has sent around the world, and what that means for the city and the level of investment

They're not market-focused, and they're scared of making dramatic changes. Their default position is: *"It's worked in the past, so we'll do that again."*

that's come into the city, is enormous. Previously, when working internationally, everybody would just talk about *Manchester United*. Now they ask: *"Which team do you support?"* (I'm a *Manchester City* fan, by the way!) It's things like that which can make a massive difference over a relatively short period of time. Yes, it still reinforces the football message, but actually, it gets people thinking in a different way.

From a perception point of view, *Manchester United* **in particular—but I assume** *Manchester City* **as well—is seen to be an internationally successful business, a brand, which just happens to be a football club. That's the difference. It's that shift where people begin to think:** *"Whoa, all right. They're a really savvy businesses."* **In some ways, this could be a hook for inward investment, because they're not just seen as a football team. They're seen as a business. I feel this is the perception being promoted now, which I imagine is helping Manchester broadly. Which goes back to the point that it can come from any angle, to promote any aspect of any destination, as long as it's articulated clearly in terms of the perception.**

Yeah, exactly. The interesting thing about *Manchester City* and the investment in the club, it's actually investment in Manchester. They are investing in a whole range of new facilities, to create this sports city around the club. It isn't just about the club and that's quite a different shift. It's also quite different to how *Manchester United* approach it.

Of course, the way *Manchester United* embraced branding, merchandising and their international markets, they really knew what they were doing. They've got a massive following all over the world. And this brings in a lot of money.

Obviously, there are a lot of true football fans who don't like the way that the football industry is going. That's a whole different conversation. But certainly, thinking more broadly about backers of football clubs investing in the city as well as the team is very interesting to watch.

I'll finish on one last question, and it's a local question for me. I was intrigued when listening to the Q&A after your talk. You were rather scathing about the positioning of Brisbane: *Australia's New World City*. **I agree it's ridiculous. But did the perception you had of Brisbane before you visited change during or after your visit?**

It's really interesting. I've been to Melbourne and Sydney a few times, but I'd never been to Brisbane or Queensland before. I asked a lot of people: *"Do you know Brisbane? Have you been to Brisbane?"* Not that many of my friends or colleagues had been, but those who had said: *"Actually, it's a really great place. I really like it."* But I didn't really have a visual picture of what the city was going to look like. I thought it would be a smaller version of Sydney—somewhere between Melbourne and Sydney, in terms of what it might look and feel like.

I was really surprised at the size of this city, which I know sounds daft. The U.K. is tiny in comparison, but I wasn't expecting Brisbane city to be as big as it is. That's maybe me sounding really parochial.

Not at all. It's validating the fact that the perception of Brisbane really is unmanaged.

I also didn't know about the wealth of the cultural offer. And I think this is something—I can't remember if I said this to you Kevin, when we spoke previously—but one thing that Australian cities do really well is embrace the waterfronts. In the U.K. we've had a tendency to turn our back on waterfronts, particularly these polluted industrial rivers and canals. But we're sorting that out. It's obviously changing now and Birmingham was the first city in the UK to see the value in embracing their canal system and making it a feature within the public realm.

It is impressive the way Brisbane has embraced its waterfront and how important that is to the life of the city. I just spent a lot of time wandering around and watching how people interacted with the place, and how important being by the river seems to be. But what was interesting is that the collection of cultural organizations [at South Bank] hasn't made a real connection with the river. It seems that their backs are to the river. I think there is an opportunity to turn that around. Of course, I don't mean physically, but to turn that around and embrace their location.

There seems to be a great cultural scene around that precinct. I was lucky to meet quite a lot of cultural practitioners. There are a lot of very good people doing very good work, and that's just not visible to us at all here in the U.K.

Having been to Sydney and Melbourne, I know the depth of the cultural offer of those cities, but we're not really aware of what's happening culturally in Brisbane. But like other Australian cities, Brisbane is really clean and feels very safe. I had anticipated that's what it might be like. Of course, the issue around the lack of public access to wi-fi was very frustrating. That does need sorting out. But it has exceeded my expectations.

Aside from your—shall we say—distaste for slogans and taglines, I find it interesting that the *Brisbane: Australia's New World City* **positioning had no bearing for you, or your experience here. In fact, it's probably null and void, if not misleading, because there's no context around it.**

I didn't know about it until I was told about it. And then when I was walking past the information center in central Brisbane, I did actually see it. But I haven't clocked it. It has no relevance as far as being something that might attract a U.K. visitor. I don't know what it means. I simply don't know what it means.

Cities can't rely on—or stop with—a slogan or a tagline. It has to be validated. It has to be communicated on multiple levels. It has to be reinforced. I truly believe branding can be incredibly dangerous because you have to live up to it, and if you don't it exposes you. You'll be found out very quickly, particularly in today's day and age. Whether or not cities employ destination branding, a slogan or a positioning line, it has to be given context, whether that's domestically or internationally. For me, perhaps one of the core take-outs from our conversation today is that cultural tourism is a long-term dialogue to provide context that will help shape a perception. And there's a lot of benefit to that approach...

Yeah. One key thing which is particularly relevant for Brisbane—in the same way it's relevant for other places that aren't capital cities—is not to compare themselves to someone else, to another city.

I've heard people say Birmingham is UK's second city. Well, it's actually not. But what does that mean, anyway—*second city*? Does anyone want to be seen as a second city? Peter Saville would always say he always thought Germany was an interesting

There's no point comparing yourself to London or Sydney or New York. It's pointless. You need to be who you are, and then as you said, Kevin, focus on how you articulate that.

example, where you had a lot of cities that were very strong in their own right. It was more equal than somewhere like the U.K., where Peter often says London is its own country now. It's almost split off from the rest of the U.K. So there's no point comparing yourself to London or Sydney or New York. It's pointless. You need to be who you are, and then as you said, Kevin, focus on how you articulate that.

Design.
Brand.
Business.

A conversation between Kevin Finn and Damian Borchok

Editor's Note: *At the time of this interview, Damian Borchok was CEO of Interbrand Australia. He is now co-founder of For The People (www.forthepeople.agency).*

Kevin Finn: To start with, you've publicly acknowledged that *Interbrand* has often been referred to as *Inter Bland* and you've responded by explaining the reason is that, historically, the network has primarily focused on strategy, but at the expense of creativity.

Damian Borchok: I think that globally the business recognizes that challenge. Over the last few years the business has been focusing more on elevating creativity. That started with the development of the manifesto around world changing brands, which has been something that's unified the business over the past few years. It's a very clear ambition that's been stated at the most senior levels; it's fundamentally important.

Generally, there was a recognition that business creativity is a growing requirement. Strategic services are valuable, and they're not diminishing in any way. But certainly there also needs to be an ability to "operationalize" those strategies, to be able to show the proof of our advice, and in the way that we make those strategies visible.

For us, this was a natural concept to follow; it's certainly something that is incredibly important. Of course, the big challenge with any shift is: Do you have the talent? Do you have the will to make the decisions that are often difficult when you're looking at changing the direction of any organization?

One of the really important aspects concerning the process of creativity is you have to be very conscious of creating the right conditions for creativity to happen. For any organization that is changing, that's one of the most difficult things to achieve, because an organization is wired in one way to do something well. If it has to be wired in another way, to do something that's different, it requires a lot of leadership, a lot of very clear thinking and commitment. It is critical to ask: What conditions are required? For creativity you need to have an environment where people are always finding sources of inspiration.

They need to be living and breathing it. They need to be having conversations with other creative people. There needs to be a natural flow to that creativity, because it isn't something you can necessarily schedule from 1:00am or 1:00pm or 2:00pm, and then expect something to pop out at the other end. It is a far

There needs to be a natural flow to that creativity, because it isn't something you can necessarily schedule from 1:00am or 1:00pm or 2:00pm, and then expect something to pop out at the other end.

more natural, organic activity. The consequence of this is that you need to be able to create an environment where this can be done effectively.

You also need to have established a very clear vocabulary within your business—a vocabulary for understanding the creativity you're trying to achieve, and how you get to it. It becomes a language that allows you to elevate creativity. If you don't have people that can have those sorts of conversations, whether they're strategists, client service people, designers, writers, or leaders of the business, it's very hard to innovate the nature of what their creativity is—and improve it.

That's obviously another challenge that needs focus. And these are things we're always conscious of. Even in our business, where we started six or seven years ago; with regards that process, it's essentially a never-ending watch.

I guess an easy way to export this throughout the *Interbrand* **network is through evidence—and there is evidence that you've achieved this, so it's not something the network is trying to figure out. The question isn't, can it work? because it's working. But in your early days, and in the context of the Australian office within the global business, I believe you were quoted as saying,** *"If we're so good, why are we so small?"* **Was that tough medicine for** *Interbrand* **to take?**

The conversations around *Interbrand's* creativity were actually held separate from what we were doing. Globally it was decided that it was important to make a change, and we came to the same conversation together. That's how it emerged. It wasn't really tough medicine, at least not from an Australian, or New Zealand point of view.

It wasn't a conversation that we ever had with the global CEO. It was something that we talked about because it was an ambition for our business. But those conversations around the business—in relation to developing creativity—was certainly something that emanated out of a global decision and which came from our CEO. It was as you've described it.

Part of achieving this is attracting big talent. In previous conversations, you've indicated there may have been a difficulty to attract that big talent, because *Interbrand* wasn't seen as a creative powerhouse, that it was seen more as a strategic powerhouse. How did you address this barrier, and what was the offer? What was the benefit for big talent to come on board?

It was a very organic process. As I've said, the previous incarnation of *Interbrand* was very much a strategic business, which had some creativity. But it was certainly not of the quality that I wanted or set the standard I expected. We needed to convince the marketplace this could change, whilst at the same time, we were only just turning the business around. There was very little evidence to demonstrate our ambitions in the marketplace, so it was probably about two years of hard work. It was very much conversation by conversation.

Internally we'd already set down the path that we weren't going to tolerate anything but a substantial lift in the way we did our creative work, and that we were not going to rest on our laurels once we thought we'd done some good work. It was very much: *"What's next? How do we elevate what we do?"* The challenge we essentially had was to present our credentials and our portfolio to every employee that potentially walked through the door, to prove to them that we were a business that was changing. It was very much a two-way conversation, rather than a one-way interview, which is often the case.

I guess we were lucky that we spent quite a bit of time with our talent consultants—who were looking for people for us—to first get candidates well calibrated in order to be able to have that first conversation, before we even met them. It was very much: *"Look, when I'm ringing up someone I know you may have a perception about Interbrand, but please you need to see them. They are changing."*

We had some really great advocates in those partners. We still do. They're all very good at being persistent where some people have questioned whether *Interbrand* was changing as a business. Once people met either myself, or our creative directors they saw that there was a genuine passion, which was supported by very clear evidence. And there wasn't just a high degree of creativity, but strategic thinking and intellect as well, which we brought to the conversation.

Because we believed in ourselves, it provided candidates with a sense of belief. We were delivering the right outcome. And more people want to be part of that. From those little conversations we were able to build up a stronger team. Then, ultimately, our work became more public. As a consequence of that, it became more recognized for what people see it is today.

It's tricky, because you really have to make hard choices early on...

Yeah, you do have to make hard choices. It requires a lot of intestinal fortitude. It requires you to be challenged about what you believe in—almost on a weekly basis. It needs to be crystal clear: *"You know what? Here's a culture that I like and I've got a really clear view about what they stand for. These are people I need to work with."* To me it is very much that kind of strength of character that I think we need to have more of in our industry.

You have a very interesting and novel way of looking at new business. You actually refer to it as an *extreme sport*. Can you expand on that?

That's probably a reaction to my personal feeling about sport. I'm not particularly into sport, generally. I know that to get balance I need to find some activity that I can compete in. I just personally like business development. It's a form of competition. For us, it is about the knowledge that—in our kind of business—we are project based and you only have so many opportunities in 12 months to win a piece of work. You have to be incredibly intense about that. There are way too many agencies. I know we get feedback from clients after we've won work, where client's have said some of the other agencies had proposals which were full of mistakes. They clearly didn't put the effort—the thinking—into it. There really wasn't the commitment.

To me, it's the opposite. You need to have the energy and the drive. You have to think about every opportunity. If you decide to go for that opportunity, then you have to put absolutely everything into it. Because you have to assume that your competitors are doing the same. You can't ever sit on your laurels reminding yourself that you've had a good run of wins and therefore you have some magic formula. It's never that easy. To me, that kind of intensity of thinking is required. If you miss that opportunity, you never get that back again. You're losing a fairly substantial opportunity. And if you lose a couple of them, you find your pipeline is declining very quickly. You've got a business that's going to be in strife.

Having a strong new business pipeline and having a strong capacity to win makes so many other problems in your business go away. You're not chasing money. You're able to hire more talent. You're able to give people pay raises. You're able to find two or three different skills to hire into the business that you didn't have before. It facilitates so many different things. It allows you to sleep at night because you're not to worrying about when the next dollar is coming through the door.

That's why it is fundamentally important to the business. A lot of people find business development quite scary and intimidating. Whilst we believe it should be intense, it should also be fun. It should be an exhilarating activity where you can ask: *"Can we trump ourselves?"* So, we review how we've done a pitch and how we actually engage a client; do we see the excitement on their faces when we talk about their business? All of those things should be an energizing experience.

I imagine there is a lot of investment within that, too.

There is a great deal of investment, and that's where the balance is really important. I've said previously we are very clear about what we choose to pitch on and what we won't pitch on because pitching does take a lot of energy. It's important to be able to choose the kind of work that you want to do, and choose the kind of opportunity to optimize that energy, and in turn to get the right work that you are best at doing.

The other side of this being like a sport is the fact that all of it can often be seen by people as a very stressful time and there is certainly intensity and stress around it. But I don't think it should be. I've seen some organizations get very tense and uptight about the pitch process and so they play a very safe game. They try to second guess. They worry about: *"How should we reduce our fee so that we win business?"* All those kind of things simply degrade the work.

The quality of the pitch is very much around how do we energize; how do we show what the future of the business is and where its potential is; and how do we excite the client by having more fun; and do we actually enjoy the opportunity to engage a client that way? When we ask: *"Should we expand on our part of the pitch?"* I think that kind of energy rubs off, in terms of how the client feels about you and the kind of experience they'll have.

I guess if you look at the extreme side of sport, it's pretty dynamic and risky. And in the case of business—and particularly in a pitch scenario—there is always a fear that the financial value, as seen by the client, is perhaps only visible through the implementation or the application of the pitched idea, rather than the idea itself being considered valuable. With this in mind, do you tend to look at pitch work as something that needs to be paid and valued, or is that incorporated into the fee if you are appointed?

Basically, we don't get involved in creative pitches and very rarely do we have a situation where there is a fee type of situation. It is more a consultative type of engagement we have around a pitch. It's typically more about us being able to demonstrate the way we can think about clients, and how we could potentially shape their business. It tends to be more around that. We focus very much on the idea of putting forth a strong point of view around a client's business first. The reason for this is partly about selection. Now, some people think if you put a strong point of view on the table straight up to the client you could end up losing them.

Our view is that: *"Yes. That's correct,"* but more importantly for us is that we need to truly believe there is a substantial problem to fix because we're not there to just make the client happy, or that it's just purely a meeting of minds. It's about us as professionals, and experts in our area of branding, and applying those skills to a category, and saying, *"Look. There is a lot broken in here that we think should be fixed. Are you up for it?"*

There are some clients that say: *"You just scared us. It seemed too overwhelming."* That's fine, because we know that when you get into a relationship with a client it is an expectation in how you pitch and how you win, and then it becomes something else. But that's a dishonest relationship. For us, we want to win work

The pitch process becomes self selecting. You get clients that you want to have, and clients that you deserve. And you get the projects you deserve, rather than just picking more work in order to get more revenue.

by clients who are inspired and excited by our perspective and occasionally say: *"You know what? We had a view about this, and these guys have been taking it to another level, or they've slightly reframed the way we thought about things. We really appreciate that kind of input. That's the kind of professional relationship we are looking for."*

In some ways, the pitch process becomes self selecting. You get clients that you want to have, and clients that you deserve. And you get the projects you deserve, rather than just picking more work in order to get more revenue because at the end of the day what you usually find is you have a disappointed team, a frustrated team, and ultimately they're stuck on a project like that for six, 12, 18 months. Often they want to go somewhere else and work on another project. They don't want to be there. I don't believe that you should be winning work under false pretenses.

A client shouldn't be appointing you under false pretenses, either. That's why the idea of the strong point of view is an incredibly important part of the conversations that we have, and hopefully through those conversations and engagements they see the value in what we do.

I guess that fits with your view of the four broad business models you've spoken about, and which you believe designers tend to fall into. Your view is there is generally some sort of trade-off within those models, which include:
1) Commodity shop.
2) Well oiled machine.
3) Product excellence firm.
4) Relationship firm.
Can you briefly expand on these and discuss which business model *Interbrand* **adopts, based on the pitch model you just described?**

Sure. The *commodity shop* is the one that I feel way too many businesses in our industry operate within. That's why there's so much conversation around: *"The clients are pushing our fees down. It's really hard to make money."* This is always a struggle for our industry. That model is based around trying to balance a whole range of things rather than having a strategic discipline and deciding: *"You know what? We're going to be good at one thing."*

Frances Frei lectured at a *Harvard Business School*, that I took. She talks about the idea of excellence. Part of her theory on excellence has been that great firms give up something. They are always going to be good at *this* and bad at *that*, because there are only limited resources you can apply. It's just not possible to be great at everything.

Similarly, take a company like *Apple*. If you've ever heard one of Steve Jobs' rare interviews, he states: *"We're a product firm. We're a product firm. We're a product firm."* That's his message. You see that in so many of the decisions they make. For me, the strategic clarity of this message is important. You'll never get out of the mire of being a commodity shop unless you make those trade-offs.

The other three are potential broad models. And of course, there may be other models. Certainly, the *well oiled* machine is the company that says: *"You know what? We want to be a high volume business. We know to do this and to make a wide market name we need to be low margin."*

But there's a consequence: *"We need to make some trade-offs. We can't attract talent because we can't pay top dollar for them. And because we need to turn things around quickly, we may have a higher staff turnover."* The consequence of that model is they make the choice and—in all likelihood— the product quality isn't as high. Not surprisingly, the client doesn't really look through the lens of quality in the same way a client who pays top dollar for design.

In fact, most of the product quality is likely to be traded off heavily. Service may need to be a little bit better to be able to smooth out some of those challenges of being a good low cost provider. That's one option.

The second one is very much the service... and that's rare. This is a firm that's actually committed to long standing client relationships. Year in and year out, they have a reasonable understanding of what kind of budgets they're going to get from clients. They're very well connected at keeping a matrix structure of relationships with the business. They have good long standing connections.

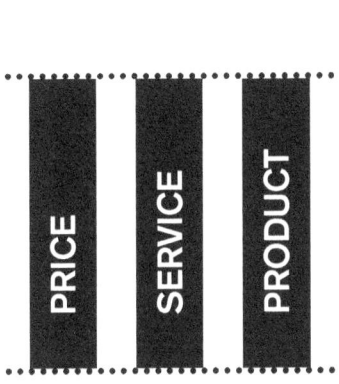
Commodity Shop

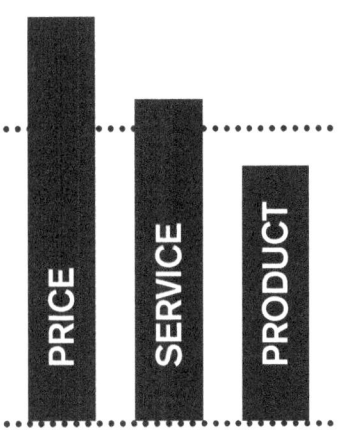
Well Oiled Machine

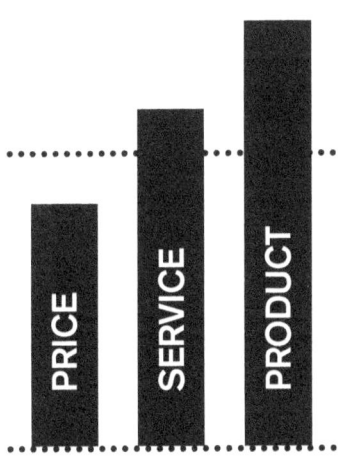
Product Excellence Firm

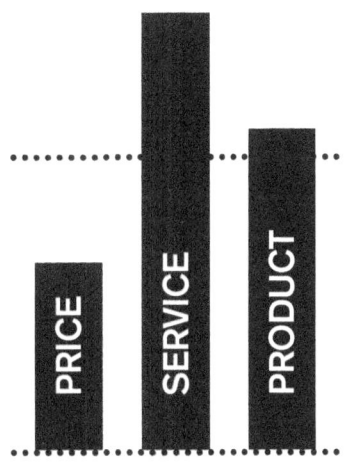
Relationship Firm

The consequence of this model is that the relationship becomes the primary choice maker for that organization. They've probably made a decision to be as good as possible by having a good relationship with a client. Difficult situations can be overcome by having relationships and this also gets you on the ground for picking up pieces of work.

The challenge lies in the nature of the work that we do. You are often dealing with quite prickly situations when you're having conversations about activity, quality of work, strategy and things like that. At some point in the relationship there's always going to be tension. Some of them can be quite scary.

Organizations that are culturally focused around relationships find those kind of tensions quite difficult to deal with, particularly if they see it as a threat to their relationship and where they'd rather remove that friction.

As an organization, what they'll often do is make a trade-off between product quality by saying: *"The client's not happy, we'll make them happy."* They'll trade off the quality of the work or they will try to mitigate risk. Doing work which is too edgy, or too radical may upset the sensibility of the client. As a consequence, they make that trade-off. Typically, that sort of organization can charge larger margins because they have that strength of relationship, particularly at higher levels. They can negotiate their position very well.

The other strength to their business is a higher degree of certainty regarding work and revenue. As a consequence, they're probably better at negotiating longer term relationships and achieving efficiencies in how they run their business simply due to that degree of certainty.

We see our business as a product business. The reason for this is we very much recognize that in the world of branding there is a lot of innovation to be done. There is a lot of development around how you use brands. And there is still a lot of uncertainty among many clients about the value that it creates.

For us, our ambition is very much based around that. Our focus is around how we show that brand isn't simply something that you stick on the top corner of the website, or on a business card,

There is still a lot of uncertainty among many clients about the value that brand and branding creates.

that it's really a time situation, that it's actually something that operates at a holistic, operational level. It is the interaction of all the touch points of your business that help drives value for your brand. As a consequence of having that view, we know that we are having a combination of educational style conversations and learning type conversations.

We have difficult conversations about why maybe some people within a closed business have a negative perception of brand—or a very out-dated view of how brand works. It often means we have to be up front about having those difficult conversations. We're also very conscious that most categories get into a rut, in terms of how they represent their brands. Give them a few years, and they all start copying each other. Everybody starts looking like one another. Even behaving like one another. They all follow the same rules. Part of our job is to break that. To break those conventions; it's one of the key tension points.

For us, it's about asking how we create the conditions where a client can come on that journey, to understand why it is better to break from the pack than to be part of the pack. That requires a fairly innovative conversation, and discussions about the way you think about how brand works.

Often we have conversations about the branding textbooks. Our feeling is that you need to be careful of what you read because clients often have the impression they have to retain things they've held for a long time. That's the way that they interpret it. We often have to show this isn't the case. The concept of brand equity dilution hasn't been talked about enough. The fact is markets change and shift, and consumers change and shift, and technology is only accelerating this.

The stuff that clients thought was an equity for them, and was valuable a couple of years ago, has now become something that is largely diluted in terms of value, in terms of changing and shaping behavior. Typically, the marketplace is ahead of that. Having those conversations is often quite challenging.

For us you can't have those conversations if you're a service type firm. For us, we need to be saying: *"We are committed to the improvement and innovation of brand. As a consequence we need to focus on the product,"* which is the kind of stuff that we provide our clients.

You mentioned earlier that clients tend to find it difficult to understand the value of brand. Economists do as well. The whole financial industry can't put a tangible value on brand. Those conversations you have with your clients, surely they have to be backed up with some sort of evidence, or proof, or some logical common sense reasoning?

That's where I'm constantly looking and we have a bit of an advantage in that, because we [*Interbrand*] value brands at a global level. We have lots of debates about: *"What makes brands successful?"* We can use this to support our arguments. And we have an analytics practice in the business, as well, where we are required to model different solutions. The way we approach it isn't running the typical focus group, or the traditional feed back targeting, because to me those are probably the most redundant, outmoded ways of looking at consumer behavior.

We rely very heavily on case studies about brands that are doing really emergent work, and which are successful. There's way too much focus on well established and mature brands who have a set pattern around what they do. They're not likely to change very much, simply because of their scale and ability to apply change capably. Their success comes from that—it's not necessarily a branding innovation that is driving their ultimate business success.

We try to look at the brands that are emerging and which are doing interesting things. We ask what that means to the future of brand. We often bring those kinds of conversations to clients. For us when you're engaging a firm like *Interbrand*, or any other branding or design firm, what you are doing is asking them to help you to innovate your brand.

To simply say: *"We are just going to polish the brand and put it back on the mantel place,"* isn't really something that's useful. That's a cleaner's job, not actually a branding firm's job. For us, we want to look at where things are changing. We build to bring your brand to your future—not to your past or your present.

From personal experience I often encounter clients asking to be re-branded, when essentially they're really looking for an *identity refresh*. One of the greatest definitions I've read between identity versus brand is from Ian Anderson

[*Designers Republic*]. **He once wrote that:** *"Identity is how you look. Brand is who you are."* **They're two totally different conversations. Do you find that clients get that distinction, or is that part of the education process?**

That is very much depending on the clients that you meet. I would still say that many, many clients—probably the majority of them—still look at the identity refresh. Those clients have managed to get some extra money within that year's budget. They haven't looked at their identity for a few years and feel it needs tidying up. The argument has been made at a fairly rudimentary level to get that additional operating expenditure, to possibly get a capex to implement. Really there aren't enough conversations yet about the *what* versus the *who*. That's partly the evolution of the Australian business landscape. It needs to focus on more advanced thinking, particularly if it wants to be competitive against the world's best.

That is the challenge, because there are more and more smart organizations with very progressive CEOs who are saying: *"You know what? This brand thing, lets put all of our focus on getting our business turned around, about how we operationalize the way we deliver services and products, and then line up brand with this and discipline the business about what we're all about."*

What we have there is not simply the brand team communicating stuff to the market about how *grand* they are, with the rest of the business disconnected from this and any success is really just serendipitous. Instead, what you have is an organization that's structured to consciously use all of the elements within its portfolio to be successful. What you're doing is implementing the delivery mechanism for the promises your brand makes. It's your identity and business model working in concert—and you end up with the proper value creation model working.

I think a lot of creatives, in particular, feel that business is dry and dull, and probably well out of their skill set. Most creatives haven't been trained in business. One of the interesting things about your situation, as CEO, is that you have a very fluid relationship with your creative director. So much so, that you can influence the direction of a creative project just by being a part of that process. That's probably

critical to collaboration and the success of what you're talking about. However, some might suggest this could be dictatorial. Should a CEO undermine a creative director and creative decisions?

Yes, I could see if I was undermining the creative director that would be dictatorial. That's certainly not the relationship that we have. Essentially, our creative directors have a real passion around our clients and the business. And this fluidness cuts both ways. We don't necessarily see there's a demarcation. You need to know the people who have particular skills, and respect them. In day-to-day work life, I'm more than happy for strategists to bleed over into creative, for creatives to bleed over into strategy. For a creative director to come to an interview with a CEO is key to understanding how their business ticks.

It's the accumulation of all of those interactions that provides far richer material. To understand that this *brand thing* isn't something that's detached from the business. The business and brand are interrelated in their ability to be able to be successful. I advocate identifying a combination of things that go on in business. I have a real passion for how business can transform and be better. I also have dismay in how often conservative—to our detriment—they can be, and how misguided, in terms of how brand is used. For me, those are the kind of energies that partly drive the business.

At the same time, I got into this industry, not because of that, but because I had a passion for design. I've spent my career trying to understand all sorts of design. I have a breadth of understanding of architecture, industrial design, and graphic design. Not only with regard to what's happening now but from an historical perspective, because it's something I have a real need to know.

Being able to do that, and being able to help facilitate other people to broaden their view of how those interactions can actually create better results—this is important to me. That's more the intent of what we're doing. I think our business is certainly heading more that way. And of course, there will be more blurred lines between all the different roles in our business. Our work changes when those crossovers happen and it becomes more interesting and more creative. I only see upside in that kind of relationship with different people.

I know of instances where CEOs became involved in the creative work and completely made a mess of things, and that's where the autocratic approach is problematic; particularly if you're a CEO that doesn't have a particularly good understanding of the creative process. The way that we work is quite different to that. I'm not going to suggest there aren't times when I say *"No. That work is not good enough. We're not taking that to the client."* That's usually in the early stages of work. We usually go through a process. We talk internally about killing ideas fast, because we need to get to the right kind of answers very quickly.

Certainly, each person that's involved in the process is there for a particular reason. Our approach is that a creative director can just as easily challenge the strategy work as much a strategist, or myself, can challenge the creative work. The key thing is that you first develop a vocabulary for what you are talking about.

There isn't much point to having a pure finance background if I'm talking about creativity, because I probably don't have any understanding of the language around it. But I've spent a lot of time studying a number of different creative industries. I've obviously worked in this industry a long time. I have a vocabulary for the kind of work that we do, and particularly my interest is around how different creative industries innovate and change—and what's leading edge.

I'm really keen to see that we bring those influences into our work just like our creative directors do on their side of the equation. Our conversations are highly collaborative. There are certain areas regarding the technique of what they do—whether it's layout, whether it's typography—that I am just completely out of my comfort zone altogether, and that's where they are extraordinary. Then there are other things, when it comes to how we link the brand and the communication with the strategy, asking how you operationalize this in the business. Because the other side of me is very much around how businesses tick.

That amounts to what I bring. It's very much around being able to bring a group of people together to have conversations about making stuff work better. In our creative process, I would probably say the first few briefs of developing a concept are almost entirely conversational.

There's almost nothing visual about it. The guys, just by nature of their work process, tend to talk their way into a solution. If they can talk about it for hours on end, and see where the potential is, they know that they can very quickly establish the visual structure for that. Once they can talk it, and convert that into a system, once they understand what that system is, it can then be tested through application—prototypes. And if it works well, that becomes the final direction.

You mentioned you went out of your way to study and understand creative language, the creative process, which is obviously hugely beneficial for the relationship you have with your team. And this is obviously in your own self interest. So is it also incumbent on the designers to understand the language of business, because generally speaking, designers tend to dislike the idea of business? In my experience, it's in a designer's best interest—and self interest—to understand business, regardless of whether they run or own a design practice. Is that something you require from your team or that you would even recommend, or suggest?

We don't expect our designers to do MBAs or anything, but I think any designer who is serious about changing organizations must have a curiosity about their client's business. It doesn't matter if it's a naive passion for it, but it's fundamentally important. I know that, for example, one of our creative directors absolutely loves having a chat with the CEO of a business. He asked all sorts of questions like: *"Why are things this way, and how does that work, and why would you do it that way? Show me why you've thought about this."* He has a very disarming way of having that kind of conversation. But when it comes to presenting the concept he's got that conversation in his head, with that level of detail about how the business works.

And you can see it's been woven from the decision making about how a concept solution works. That makes for a fairly powerful conversation, because they are talking about how this works for your business, rather than engineering a concept.

It provides a much stronger foundation to clients for believing in the solution, and if you're willing to present a more dramatic or challenging solution to the client it offsets some of the tension or nervousness about risk.

We don't expect our designers to do MBAs or anything, but I think any designer who is serious about changing organizations must have a curiosity about their client's business.

By the time you are at creative director level if you are not prepared to have those kinds of conversations with a client—simply believing the brief should have all you need, and your creative genius will save the day—you're out of touch.

That kind of creative director is so old school, and we never want to have one like that, because businesses are so complex, and the issues that you are dealing with, if you are seriously looking deeply into the brand of a client, you really need to have your sleeves rolled up. Otherwise, you're not going to deliver a solution that has any sustainable advantage for them.

Nor will you be speaking a similar language.

Yes. You're talking design language, and the client will end up asking someone to translate that for them. Our creative director talks a lot about having a mathematical logic so the client can see how you've come to your solution, because we know most organizations tend to be less brand orientated. You need to be quite sequential in your thinking; even though your creative process might have been more systemic. You need to then lay out your answer in a way that they will be able to lead effectively.

It also paves the way for intuition, because it is supported by logical, business-oriented thinking. You're not just relying purely on intuition: *"This works. Trust me."* **And when intuition** *is* **introduced, this process has paved the way in the client's mind where they are more open to intuitive decisions, because it is backed up and supported by other decisions that are much more logical, much clearer, and communicated in a way that is common business language. Would that be correct?**

That's right. And with this they should be able to ask advice. We typically look at the problem from an evolutionary point of view and explore how to then synthesize the solution, and I believe that is an incredibly important combination. I think being purely analytical gives you very dull solutions, and being purely focused on the simplicity of something without any connection to the real world you end up inside a very strange place where your success is often serendipitous. You might have a meeting of minds with the client, but it's not necessarily connected to any substance. It is very much the combination of those components working together that get you the right outcome for the client.

I guess it's seen as a grey area in the client's mind because they are expecting to navigate a designer's intuition, and that's probably a frightening situation for many people who are embedded in the business world.

Yes. There are so many designers but when we have conversations with them there are so few we would hire, because when you ask them how they came to their solution they can't give you an answer. They can't articulate the process. There is another thing that many designers talk about: *their work should speak for itself.* To me, that's an abdication of their responsibility, and an easy way to avoid providing a clear answer for their rationale.

The problem is they have no discipline around developing an idea first. That's why I said earlier that our creative directors will talk about the solution from day-to-day-to-day, until they get to that point, because what they are doing is essentially disciplining their mind around an idea.

For me, I don't like clients being annoyed and cynical if they need to decode a concept or figure out how you arrived at the solution, what the reasons are and why the elements are put where they are. If you don't have a story that is supported by a logic I don't think you have a solution of any substance.

I know people often say: *"it's a systematic process that you don't understand,"* but that is a cheap way out. I don't really buy that.

Switching the conversation a little bit, with such a volatile and unpredictable economic climate and with perhaps diminishing client budgets as a result, how financially viable are large studios or large networks—as opposed to a group of smaller, independent studios that might be a collaborative force?

I think we'll always have both. In my experience it comes and it goes in waves. I remember when there was a big move towards big global brand businesses; they had a certain expertise. Then, a number of clients began thinking: *"Actually, they're expensive, they're a bit slow. In reality we have a relationship with a subset of that group—who are our team. At the end of the day, they kind of look like a small business."* Eventually, some of those little teams often start their own businesses. The big client follows them, and more clients pick that up.

I think we certainly see some of that—this agility thing, and the speed of being in the small agency. If you have some really top talent, if you focus that talent around a couple of top clients, you can do really well.

It switches back, because a lot of those businesses then recognize that when they start up, they might have a fresh new client, there's energy, but then they get caught up in a lot of the management. How do you deal with growth? *"Do I have the infrastructure to deal with finance and IT and all the other things if I bring a big client across?"*

It starts to break down. A couple of people might leave. You bring in some other people. All of a sudden the quality of the firm declines. The client says, *"FYI, it's not really working. I'm going back to B agency."*

You get these waves of changes. To me, I don't see scale as really being the driving force around quality and results. I think there are a lot of really great small businesses and there are really, really cool big ones, too. There are really crappy small ones and really crappy big ones. There's no correlation between size and quality of the work that you get.

It's very much around how is the business is being led? Who's the talent in the business? How progressively minded are they in the way that they are improving their products and the way that they can serve their clients? It's those kind of questions that you think about to find whether an organization is going to do great creative work for you or not.

I guess there's a perception that growth means you have to get more staff, get bigger clients, and that produces a need to 'feed the machine.' Then it's difficult to be selective in deciding on client work to accept. This begins to cannibalize your position because you're just trying to pay the bills. Now, that's one perception of growth. You've personally experienced growth at *Interbrand***, from just a few people to quite a large organization. How have you navigated that growth so that it doesn't begin to impact the product?**

In the back of your mind you always have to ask: *how sustainable is big?* That's often a challenge. There's a real fear, particularly if you're in a business that has to achieve monthly targets in order to get there. Does that dysfunctional behavior force compromise, or chasing the dollar? That is always a balancing act. From our experience, I would say that, in Sydney, it's a much bigger market than anywhere else in Australia. You can sustain a decent size studio, probably 30 or 40, maybe on a good day 50, people with what I would call a standard consulting service.

One approach is identifying the great business you did and just doing more of the same. But some organizations ask themselves how they can extend those relationships with other things and get deeper in the relationship.

The other option is you add new products. That's the important thing for us. The product firm is really the key. Motion graphic business is certainly a few years old but doing well. Verbal identity is growing. Employee engagement programs and team is vital too. They started to expand after about 18 months of hard work in finding the right sort of relationships to do that kind of work.

That allows us to have a fairly stable and traditional strategy and design group, but the other parts of the business that we add on are new. New types of work that we're doing is adding new value to the business and allowing us to grow.

The other thing with the brand globally isn't simply about the size of the office, or the geographic spread of the service. Sydney has grown to a particular size. Melbourne has a lot more opportunity to advance the business.

To me it's still very early days for that part of the business, in terms of its opportunity. Growth can significantly expand that office in the coming year. There are different ways that you manage growth. There are some ways you can chase the dollar. To me that's not sustainable, because sure enough somewhere along the track, you're going to lose a client, or there's going to be another GFC [Global Financial Crisis]. You have a big, lumbering business that's got a long way to fall.

I guess the two sides of that coin are: *Diversify* **and, if you refer back to something that you mentioned earlier, to** *be good at one thing as opposed to being a generalist.* **Is there a danger when you start adding new products and expanding your business? It achieves diversification, but do you then have to walk that fine line by being very clear about what you do?**

Yes. That can be a challenge. We usually expect about a three year lead-time before it actually gets real traction, because you have all those classic innovation curve events. There may be a few clients who are early adopters. They might take it on. Some of them might question the experience you've got in a new area for the business. They might question how good your team is. They might think: *"I have never heard Interbrand doing this sort of stuff locally before. Is this real?"* Those are probably a more mass market kind of client, and so they will wait for a couple of years. You have to be quite mindful of that. If you build a product, go to market and think that it didn't take off this year, you are leveling the opportunities on the table.

The other point is that we don't play that generalist game. We are essentially a large office of specialists. We are very much focused on hiring people who have specific skills. Like, for example, with our environments people they are interior designers and architects.

Hiring a person whose career has been built in that area, and has that expertise, that's a very different conversation to your marketing department, for example. Those kind of perspectives enrich the business, as well as actually provide us with the credibility that we need.

I guess a softer way to introduce those new products would be to offer those new services to your existing clients so you can say, *"This is something else—within the remit of our project with you. But we can also do this new service."* **That way you're not going to the market with a whole new pitch to new clients...**

Yeah. You can sometimes have those wins, and that's good if you have the trust of your client, but then you have other clients that you've worked with for a long time who have a very fixed view of what they have hired you for, and they just will not accept that you do anything else. We do. We have those challenges quite a bit. They hire us for our strategic thinking, and they have a very blind view of all the other things that we can do. Sometimes they are the ones that take the longest to come around. It is horses for courses. You do get a mix on that front.

***Interbrand* is part of the *Omnicom Network* so with the *Publicis Omnicom* mega merger, does this development impact the business structure at all? Does it put extra pressure or add**

KPIs, or change the business focus? Or, is it more of a positive addition to the service that you can provide? *[Editor's Note: This interview took place before the Publicis Omnicom merger collapsed.]*

It's really hard to say at the moment. It's a merger that has been stated, but there's a whole bunch of things that have to happen before it becomes official. At this stage, there's no change as far as I can tell. We're 'business as usual' for the minute. I'll probably wait and see what becomes of it. I haven't been through one of these large scale mergers before so I'm not really sure what to expect. Because these acquisitions tend to be lots of businesses that are part of a portfolio coming together they tend to go about their business— unless there's some crossover.

Obviously, there are scale opportunities and things like that, and there are probably some competitive advantages. It's still certainly very early days to fully understand the implications.

Some could argue that, with this kind of super power mega merger, it might create a less creative landscape. Would you agree with this assessment?

It was Martin Sorrell who made that point. But no, I don't necessarily think there's a correlation between scale and creativity. It's often an argument that you could become less creative, but I don't buy that argument. There are plenty of really rubbish small firms, as well. There are plenty of good, big firms. It comes back to the conditions that you create to deliver creativity. No, I don't agree that's going to be an issue.

We see the rise of the smaller, independent studio. It's an increasing trend at the moment, but do you think it might galvanize the smaller independents or at least increase the number of them?

It may, certainly. It's always interesting when you have a major shift in the market. The smaller studios work to fill that in, because the emergence of more small, creative agencies is probably a cool thing to have happen. The more new things that are happening in a marketplace the more it provides a better dynamic, a better sense of competitiveness. The interesting thing around the emergence of the smaller agencies is a response to a particular shift that's happening—the need for organizations to be more agile, more creative, more adaptive.

Smaller agencies are certainly meeting that challenge. We often talk about the war for talent. In our industries, it can often take a bunch of talented mavericks to come together, and they've got a very new, exciting product.

The thing that I find interesting about this is the challenge this sets and how you renew yourself. How do you refresh yourself? And how do these other players set benchmarks? You then have to think about: *"If we're a leader, we need to think about that context."* And also ask: *"What does leadership mean for our kind of business?"*

These are the kinds of things that I find interesting. I actually like a marketplace with that kind of dynamic. Apart from keeping me on my toes, I think it keeps everybody fresh—if they actually want to be successful.

You mentioned earlier that one of the products, which *Interbrand* has developed—and a term *Interbrand* may have coined—is the term *verbal identity*. Can you expand on that?

Verbal identity responds to what branding identity does, in relation to the graphic side of things. But there is a whole bunch of other things you can think about. Language is one. I know sound is becoming more popular. The nature of touch, and particularly when it comes to user experience and interface is now becoming something to consider as a more important dimension of emotionalizing, and creating a sensory experience around a brand.

To come back to the idea of 'verbal identity,' A number of years ago there was a guy called John Simmons, who worked at *Interbrand*. He ran a language practice within the London office, and he wrote a number of books. The one that I read was called *The Invisible Grail,* which certainly stuck in my mind as being one of the more interesting business books, which I often find really boring and formulaic for the most part.

But this one is really exciting, because he opened my mind to the idea of language, and he was probably one of the real pioneers of this field. Whilst we've had copywriters for years and years as a key part of brand communication, nobody actually thought of establishing 'verbal identity' as a product when building visual brands.

We often talk about the war for talent. In our industries, it can often take a bunch of talented mavericks to come together, and they've got a very new, exciting product.

This has been something *Interbrand* has been doing for many years. It makes a lot of sense, when you start to think about how brand guidelines usually consist of many hundreds of pages of visual expression. When you get to the verbal identity part, you usually have about two or three pages. But if you consider the amount of interactions that you have with a brand, whether it's spoken, or with a specific language, that's a very disproportional representation in your guidelines document.

For us, it's a fundamentally important piece of what we offer and how people communicate your service. For example, it's important for when somebody in a call center talks on the phone. But it also involves looking at how you write. Given the extent of social media, and how it is such a language-based medium, this is really key.

Anybody who reads literature will be aware that certain writers have their own kind of voice. Why wouldn't a brand have its own tone of voice? When we refer to tone it isn't just about a list of things like: *"Keep it simple, use straightforward language, be friendly and engaging."* It's about finding a style that's all your own.

One great example I use is a gym in Utah called *Gym Jones*. They have such a strong tone of voice, and you can see that it's come from the leader—and the passion of that leader. It's an extreme gym, and only the most elite athletes go there.

They talk about this on their home page and their tagline is *The Art of Suffering.* They state they are exclusive—and that they exclude. They say you can expect to have mental and physical breakdowns there. There are no mirrors in the gym. There is no air conditioning. You have concrete floors, and it's hard work. There is an intensity and brutality to their attitude and their language represents the experience you have. This is a very honest, true representation of the tone of that business, all delivered through its language. It's a hugely successful business. Anyhow, you're left with no confusion about what you are going to get. I think more brands need that kind of clarity. Perhaps not in that style, but certainly understanding the world that you want to build, and how people want to see that world.

This is not simply dumbed down by the legal department, and a boring 2000 word lexicon of business speak, which is what most organizations present. Just go to most corporate websites and you can see that the same repetitive, jargonistic language is there.

It's interchangeable...

It's created to cause anonymity and to ensure that, essentially, it flattens out the experience you have with the organization so there are no bumps along the way. The result is that you are left with a characterless organization—and an absence of branding their language.

I guess, in many ways, it refers back to the point we discussed earlier about the pitch process where, oftentimes, the pitch process becomes self selecting. Verbal identity helps that self selection, in terms of who you might attract. For example, the gym you gave as a case study, they will attract a particular kind of person who is looking for that experience. It is self selecting.

Absolutely! They know exactly who they want. They don't want some 20 something that just wants it to be cool and hip. They want somebody who is an elite athlete and they're obviously clearly positioned that way. It may not work as a mainstream proposition— it probably wouldn't—but for them that's absolutely spot on.

It's a niche market. They know exactly what to do, what they want to do, and I'm sure they have included within their language that it's not just about the brutality of the experience, but also the benefit, the outcome.

Absolutely. Yeah. You get the full leadership piece that they have on their site about the kind of development and how they grow their people. Everything is pretty extraordinary. You can see the whole package, in terms of this intensity and brutality on one side, but you also see yourself coming out the other end as the best person you expect to be.

You've mentioned *'innovation'* a few times, and in a recent conversation we briefly discussed the issue of innovation and its potential overuse in the context of business expectations. My view is that true innovation is a game changer, and usually only happens over a longer period of time. You

argue that the idea of innovation can actually be a language tool, which can be used regularly to specifically leverage or persuade in a client situation. Can you expand on this?

It very much comes down to whether you want to narrowly or broadly define the nature of innovation. It's not so important to me. I probably use the term as a short-hand because there are lots of different types of innovation. There is business model innovation. There is service innovation, client innovation. There's all sorts of ways to actually cut that conversation up. For us, the idea that innovation needs to be something big isn't the case, because innovation can be evolutionary by its nature.

You don't necessarily come to an end, but we see the exploits and end results of innovation, and usually those innovations are a consequence of months, years, decades of evolution, and work, and thinking. That's why I probably have a wider view of it. I know when you look back on the history of branding it has evolved, but it has been done through certain individuals and organizations who question the way branding works and find a better way of looking at it, which actually moves things along.

That is part of the innovation process; even though it may look quite glacial over time. There are categories that should be considered as innovation, other than just the new product they want to launch, or the new service that they are going to do. Instead, they need to look at the way they think about their category, the way they think about how their business is run, the way that they interact with each other as potential sources innovating the nature of their firm and their behavior to actually deliver new results.

I have a wider definition, because I find it helpful to consider how you bring about change, and the ongoing effects as this can be quite substantial. Even though, initially, they might come from quite small things.

Is that something you actively put into context for people? Because there is the sense that innovation, or a start-up mentality, is the new buzz, or the most recent buzz phrase within business, and people expect to be innovating every other week. In terms of when you use the term 'innovation,' is it within the context of what you just described?

The idea that innovation needs to be something big isn't the case, because innovation can be evolutionary by its nature.

What I've just talked about it is within that context, but I think there is a dangerous trap companies who hire 'innovation experts' can fall into by sticking them in a corner with certain expectations put upon them. Not surprisingly nothing happens, because they weren't connected with all the things that work in the business and which were required to actually deliver the innovation.

They hire companies that are really great at consulting on how innovation can be done. The meetings are really fun and feel like great entertainment and emotionally inspiring. But at the end of the day when they return back to the business they recognize they couldn't make any of this stuff, because the firms were great about inspiration, but they really avoided the fact that you have to operationalize innovation.

That's where the hardest part comes in. I hate the idea of trying to create the big, explosive results in a disconnected way with a business. I've often had clients say to me: *"Now, we need to think out of the box."* That's when I say: *"Here we go again!"*

Out of the box is disconnective thinking, so I say to clients: *"You've got to stop thinking out of the box. You need to think inside the box. The problem with you people is that your box is too bloody small, and what you need to do is create the conditions in the business to be better at creating those new things. If you don't do that, you're going to be stuffed."*

A few years ago I read a really interesting thing about *Pedigree*. Before they did anything they spent a lot of time in the organization looking into the things they needed to change. A lot of that was very much around: *"You know what? Why aren't there any pets in this office?"* It was as simple as that. How do you have an empathy for your end customer if you don't actually allow them in the office?

Its understanding how you create those conditions for creativity and innovation first, and whether you can actually create sustainable behavior in the business around that. It isn't a one-off event, and you might have one little bit of success. It needs to by systemic to be real.

So it's absolutely cultural. It also relates to a phrase Ji Lee (who also features in this issue) uses: *"Ideas are nothing, doing is everything."* **That's the follow though you're talking about, right?**

Yeah. For too many organizations, it's very easy to analyze and strategize when you're sitting in meetings. But the real talent in your business is those people who actually get down to doing the stuff, those that know how to do things. That's what more organizations need. I think this will happen, because we are starting to see the emergence of more and more metrics around employee behavior. I think as technology develops, and big data becomes more widely used in the way business works, we will see a lot more evaluation on who is doing what, when, where, how— and how they are going to get outcomes.

That will shine a very stark light on these kinds of dysfunctional behaviors around not actually doing stuff in business. That's a pretty exciting thing to see happen, because often companies don't react to the culture of *not doing* by saying: *"We need to be more entrepreneurial, and we need to be the leader,"* and all that sort of stuff.

Which is correct, but often there is a misunderstanding in the nature of this, because entrepreneurship is often seen as *cowboy*, and *radical*, and *fly-by-night*. We need to pick out the right characteristics from that behavior because here is an operational skill these people have that is really important to our business, and that's what we need to introduce, creating conditions for that to work effectively.

Earlier you mentioned how branding—or the brand landscape—has changed over time; market driven, technology driven, etc. A recent development within the branding field is *dynamic identities*, **and I know** *Interbrand* **has developed a number of dynamic identities, which are identity systems with numerous variations of a logo or a visual theme. In an interview on** *Design Boom* **Michael Bierut [***Pentagram***, New York] proposed that the popularity of dynamic identities will decline. He states:** *"Looking at 10,000 logo variations is entropic and exhausting."* **He goes on to say:** *"on the other hand there is something so calm and comforting about a fixed, enduring symbol upon which people can impose their own private interpretations there. The dynamism happens in the real world in a more natural way."* **Do you agree with this prediction, and also his assessment?**

I probably agree with a lot of what he says. But I don't think it'll be as absolute. I think he is completely right that it is faddish.

Will it return to stability? For some organizations, yes. I think they'll make that choice. They will probably feel having 300 different versions of their logos is too hard to manage. The thing is, though, when you look at the degree of change in technology it's not slowing down. And it's just going to get faster and faster. Things are more dynamic. They change with a high degree of regularity. We have more touch points. We have more points of interaction. We've reached more people. There is a need for dynamism that I don't think will go away.

Now, with dynamism you also need to have stability. Otherwise, people end up being disoriented in all that they see. His point of view about having that kind of stability does make sense.
One of the various essentials to understand is that language is a dynamic thing. Is your language the element that changes? You don't have to have your visual side change as much, but certainly it's a mix of a range of things that will occur. The fact that we are moving more towards a video database world, which is only bigger and more expansive, means we will see identities evolve again—not necessarily return to where they were, but certainly evolve.

We are starting to see that *Microsoft* and *BBC* have done work around this intersection between brand interaction design, experience, and user interface. That's a really interesting development where it's no longer the design of your identity, and then separating the design of an interface.

It's the two of those coming together to create one, and for me it's a wider idea of the concept of design working holistically in the business to create an experience. That is often why it's actually going to be a more dynamic experience. It will breed new waves for considering these intersection points, and the way brands work will have more interesting functionality in how they represent brand to people.

Will that relate to logos? I'm not so sure, but I think certainly the other design elements that you create will become just as important, because they are part of the operating system of your business. That's a really cool development. I am more interested in that than worrying about whether it's going back to static logos, or whether we going to have more dynamic identities, because it's neither here nor there, really.

There are other sides to the brand of communications that can be dynamic. In a conversation I had with Peter Saville [Open Manifesto #4] we discussed developments in branding. His view was that a key thing for a brand is that it must be a regular, frequent news generator. If it's not generating news, it gets clipped out of our awareness, and the news that it generates must be 'on message.' That could be a space for dynamism. Would you agree with that? If so, does the fact of being a news generator depend on the size and the nature of the brand in question?

I can certainly agree with that point. I think brand identity is often created for purposes of anonymity, and at best they are often created just to be a signpost for an organization. That's all that they do. They don't play an active role in shaping and influencing people's behavior, and often organizations make the compromising assumption that it's about creating perception, and I don't buy that. You don't get a result on perception. You get a result on behavior.

Therefore, if you believe that brand has a role in shaping people's behavior, you need to first understand what behavior you want to shape and influence. You need to know what the brand needs to do. Your concept of newsworthiness is fundamental. It means your brand has to be on the front foot.

And you have to have a point of view. It has to have something to say where people actually want to sit up and take notice. I think all of those things are hallmarks of really great brands. That would be a fundamental part of brand performance. It's a sign of confidence about knowing who you are and what you want to do, and being able to engage and shape the way people think about the world, and how they think about you as an organization. All of those things are good things.

Of course being a news generator—or being within the wider consciousness—does help with perception. Even though you dismissed perception earlier, it is a valid concern for a lot of people where perception may be nothing near reality. When perception is more visible than reality then perception plays a huge role as a news generator.

I think brand identity is often created for purposes of anonymity, and at best they are often created just to be a signpost for an organization.

Yes. My view around perception is that it's part of the journey, but it's not the end result. Also, many organizations are still happy to look at evaluating perception but not actually getting to the hard questions regarding to what degree they are influencing behavior. Behavior is certainly influenced by perception. That's what I mean. It's part of the way on the journey. At the end of the day, this is where so much cynicism comes around design projects and marketing activities because most CEOs, CFOs, and COOs are saying: *"You know what? My sales team have told me I've sold about 10 percent more than I did last year. What's our marketing telling me? We've increased perception by X percentage points, and that some of our attributes are performing better than they were last year, right? But tell me how this is actually changing people's behavior to get a result."*

That's where the results-based view of branding needs to become a far more behavioral-based view where branding speaks for more than simply 'perceptions' management, because with perceptions management you are only doing part of your job.

It's about operationalizing the brand. Understand, for example, how brand can play a role in improving the way your front line staff actually engage customers because that prompts comments like: *"You know what? These front line staff are actually influencing buyer behavior."*

It's through our ability to shape the way they improve their service and get access to their behavior, where I can actually show my brand activity is doing something. It's those kinds of things that are particularly interesting, and if you want to do the hard job of providing real facts around what brand can do, that's the stuff that you need to be thinking about rather than simply how can my communications move perception.

I'll finish on this question, which comes off the back of what we've just discussed, and it's in relation to perception. There is a lot of public pressure for organizations to engage in corporate, social, and environmental responsibility, and in a conversation that I had with Wally Olins [Open Manifesto #5] around this topic he stated: *"If a commercial organization believes that it will be in its interest to become charitable, I don't want to sound cynical here, but the appropriate phrase is lacking self interest. If they see it as being in their interest to be socially responsible, then that is what they will do, and that is a very powerful mechanism for change."*

Generally speaking, do you feel that we are at a point where most organizations do see the benefit of this—beyond their own self interest—or are we still in that marketing spin stage?

I think some organizations are in different stages of evolution. It's part of the innovation curve. There are some that very quickly adopt it and fully embrace it, and fundamentally understand it. There are others that say: *"You know what? A few people have done that sort of thing, and it seems to be the right thing to do so we'll adopt it."* And there are others that will be unrepentant in saying: *"Absolutely no. This is nonsense. I don't see any upside. We are in this to make more sales, and we are going to stay focused. We are going to stay lean and mean around that."* You are always going to have these various states of organizational evolution.

I guess the wider consideration—and it's the thing that's most compelling for me around this whole conversation—is that it's leading us to a place which is far more interesting and far more important in the nature of the role of organization in society. Historically organizations are always seeing themselves as something apart from society. They are almost like this old garden in which commerce is conducted, very much about creating shareholder value, and where they set their own operating rules and rhythm, feeling they should be allowed to just get on with that.

I think economics is a fundamental engine of any society. The participation of business in, not only the economics of that society but also the welfare and the way that we live, is fundamentally important, because they influence degrees of employment. Organisations create a mechanism for commerce to happen. They create wealth that influences the degree to which you can have a healthy colorful sector or not-for-profit sector. It's a consequence of all these interactions that the businesses can't see themselves as being separate, and are largely compliant to the rules of the country, but where they are essentially setting their own rules on a day-to-day basis. They are a fundamental part of the fabric of society, and therefore their role is to operate an organization that is part of a full society. To me, that's the interesting piece.

This will ultimately evolve into a general requirement for organizations to demonstrate they are playing a role in society

The participation of business in, not only the economics of that society but also the welfare and the way that we live, is fundamentally important, because they influence degrees of employment.

as opposed to seeing themselves as separate from it. And I think that will shape the way decisions are made around how organizations behave at a day-to-day cultural level—and how that can be more pervasive. Organizations will be free to choose the degree to which they proactively provide more connections.

It's also generational, because we tend to forget that organizations are filled with people. The generation that is coming up now, and those following behind them—have much more social, cultural, and environmental awareness, and those people who go into those organizations won't just be expected to have this type of view. This is the view they already have, and I think, perhaps, what you are predicting will happen purely because of the people who are in those organizations.

You're probably right about that. I think it will take perhaps maybe another generation or two for them to be more pervasive. It certainly will evolve that way. I think we still have the equivalent of—what might be referred to as—the DNA of the Industrial Age, which is evident in some businesses, though that is certainly disappearing. We are seeing, at almost every level of decision influence, how workplaces are shaped, or the nature of the way you conduct business, and the degree of collaboration, and we are about to see more organizations driven by purposes rather than processes. All these kinds of things are markers toward that evolution.

I think it will be a matter of time because all the particularly big organizations are slow to change, due to the scale of those demands. You do need a generational change to actually bring about those kinds of significant cultural shifts.

Are you optimistic?

Oh, yeah! I am always optimistic. You can't not be, because part of the job is walking into businesses facing a lot of challenges, and you have to be thinking: *"How can make them the best that they can be?"* By the very nature of what we do we have to be optimistic about it, because we like fixing stuff.

Self-interest Exam for Graphic Designers

An exercise by Jason A. Tselentis

Answer the following questions by selecting the best answer. There is only one correct answer per question.

1. At the university:

a. I majored in art;
b. I majored in design;
c. I majored in art and then switched to design because I wanted to make money;
d. Answers "*a*" and "*b*";
e. None of the above.

2. When taking on paid freelance projects or personal projects, outside of the workday schedule:

a. I do them to earn enough money to purchase the next *iPhone*;
b. I do them even though I don't want to do them, but I really want the next *iPhone* so I do them with a grudge, but am excited about the money and the next *iPhone* I'll be able to get with the money;
c. Answer "*b*" with "new apps" replacing "the next *iPhone*";
d. From time to time I have taken on freelance projects that are pro bono (for good) and do them for free (donating my time) or as an exchange (perhaps getting something else in return that's not necessarily money);
e. I rarely take on additional work because I am so busy and dedicated to the work I already have.

3. When doing personal work, outside of the normal workday schedule:

a. I call it art;
b. I call it design;
c. I call it play;
d. I think personal work is stupid and no designer should do such a thing;
e. I don't care what it's called; I'm just compelled to do it.

4. In choosing what clients to work with, which of these matters most?

a. Doing good work for the client;
b. Caring about the client;
c. Caring about the client's audience;
d. What the client cares about;
e. All of the above.

5. True or False? I am happy with my portfolio.

a. True;
b. False;
c. I've never been happy with it;
d. I don't have a portfolio, I show my work on my website or my *iPad*.

6. In the *Simplified Design Process Graphs* (SDPS) opposite, which representation most closely resembles your own start to finish process with moments of happiness and disgust from the beginning to end?

a. Graph A;
b. Graph B;
c. Graph C;
d. Graph D;
e. None of the above.

7. When I take on client work that yields more income, and I find myself making more money:

a. My level of bliss increases;
b. My level of bliss stays the same;
c. I find myself suffering more panic attacks, and sleeping less;
d. I'll tell you what's blissful: Not having to work! At all!!!

8. When taking on a client, which of these metrics primarily guides a decision to take them on or not?

a. Creative reasons;
b. Financial reasons;
c. Personal reasons.

Charts Accompanying Question 6

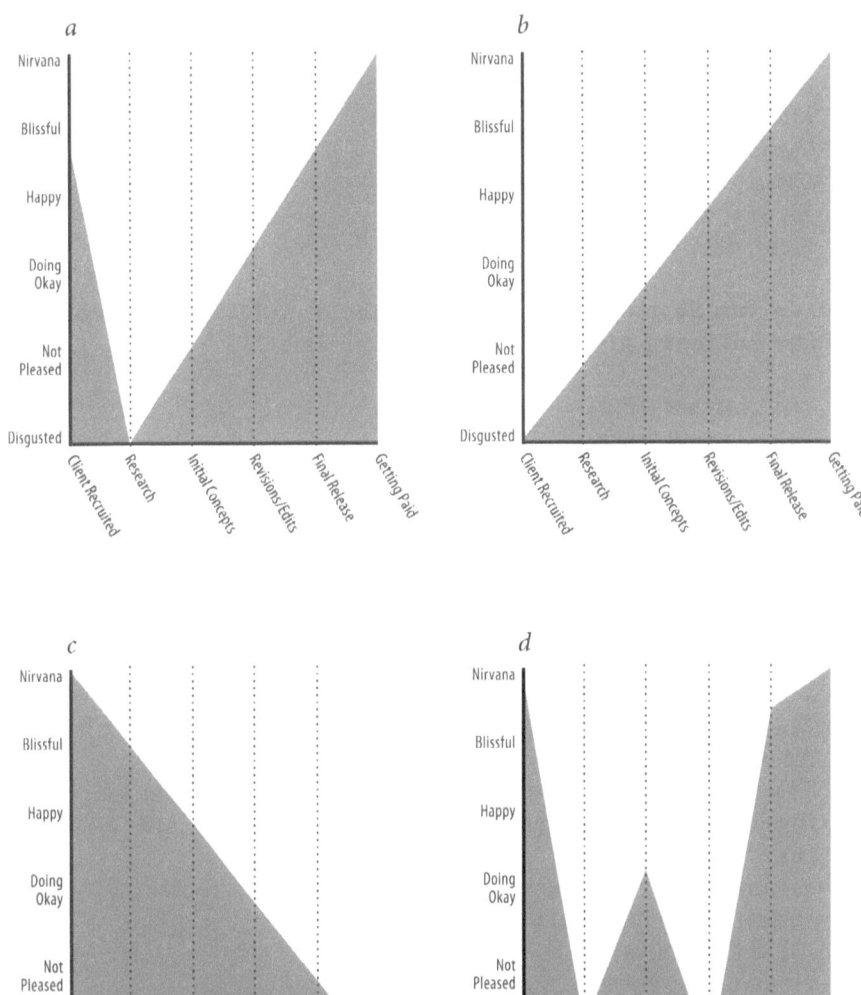

9. I consider my work to be:

a. Graphic design;
b. Design;
c. Advertising;
d. Marketing;
e. Visual communication;
f. Visual communication design;
g. All of the above;
h. None of the above.

10. As you develop your design business and portfolio, which of the following gives you the most pride?

a. Winning awards;
b. Doing good work;
c. Being respected by your peers;
d. Making money;
e. Being able to sleep at night;
f. Fuck pride.

11. The worst part of doing design work is:

a. The client;
b. The deadlines;
c. Answers "*a*" and "*b*".
d. The backstabbing account executive at my office that has terrible taste in typography and takes the client's side all the time;
e. Sitting in front of a computer in a chair that wrecks my thighs, back, and buttocks;
f. All of the above;
g. None of the above.

12. At design conferences, or any other place where you co-mingle with fellow designers, do you:

a. Remain stand-offish about work-related matters, choosing to talk about sports, the *Kardashians*, *The Real Housewives* of wherever, *Breaking Bad*, *Homeland*, or any other pop culture or entertainment instead of the design work I'm doing because my business is my business;

b. Talk about work-related design matters, but keep it to just "design in general," without getting into specifics, especially avoiding my own business, clients, and office's economic issues;

c. Design conferences? Who needs that shit?

13. You have a mortgage, two car payments, $5,000 on your credit card, and three children you need to feed, shelter, and put through school, plus your dog needs to begin taking medication that costs $100 per month. If 80% of your existing client work dried up, and disappeared, but a socially and morally irresponsible company approached you to do work that would help you recover your lost business and wages, what would you do?

a. Take on the immoral work as soon as possible;

b. Not take the immoral work.

14. You took on a risky client that does social and economic good, and you produced well-designed materials for them over the years that won you awards; eventually the client goes out of business and is unable to pay you the remaining money for work you've done. How do you respond?

a. Not hold a grudge, and just move on because they only owe 20% of the total billable hours, and that's worth the price since I won plenty of awards;

b. See if they'll give me some of their office furniture, since they won't need it any more and I really liked a couple of the chairs and desks they had. If they don't give it to me as payment, I'll take it anyways—along with other materials that amount to the 20%—as a lien on the balance due;

c. I sue them;

d. I would have never have let this happen because I always conduct due diligence with a full background check and review of a potential client's financial history and net worth;

e. I reconsider why I'll take on clients in the future—especially risky ones—and give less consideration to so-called "good will" (whether social or economic) and "award potential."

Answer Key and Further Reading
Give yourself one point for each correct answer, unless otherwise noted.

1. d
If you answered "*e*" then don't feel bad. Many designers (even great ones) didn't go to the university to study their practice. However, under traditional/older definitions, one would call design a commercial art; and by Rand's design definition (see answer and notes to question 9) design has "multiple definitions" so answers "*a*" and "*b*" are both design. Anecdotally, the author has heard answer "*c*" from his students for as long as he's been a teacher (since 1999), and he himself made the switch from art to design not necessarily to improve his chances for steady wage-earning, but mostly because he would have majored in design first had he known that you could study design in college in the 1990s; high school guidance counselors at the time were not privy to graphic design, they just knew it was done on computers, which they called "the tan boxes with keyboards, a mouse, and a printer that you used to make flyers and brochures, and stuff like that."

2. e
See Stephen Darwall's "Self-Interest and Self-Concern" pages 165–167 from *Self-Interest: Volume 14, part 1*, and his reference to *Moral Thinking* by R.M. Hare where in pages 101-106 Hare gives background on "now for then" and "then for then" motivations. If you answered "*d*" hopefully you strive to get something—don't work for free. *Pro bono* does not necessarily mean "for free" it means "for good" so if you thought all along that pro bono *had* to mean "for free" then give yourself -10 points for this question whether or not you answered it correctly. See the AIGA's stance on *pro bono* and *for free*. (http://www.aiga.org/position-spec-work/)

3. e
Jean Baudrillard's *Selected Writings*, edited by Mark Poster from Stanford University Press in pages 106–108 suggests that work is work and play is play, as culled from Marxist philosophy. If you answered "*d*" then fine but no need for name calling; also see Adrian Shaughnessy's *How to Be a Graphic Designer Without Losing Your Soul* 2nd edition, where pages 117-118 cover the "self-initiated brief" and how designers best operate, whether *responding to* or *creating* a brief.

4. a
When considering Aristotle's ruler-ruled principles, the soul should be the principle-guiding element, and one's work is closest to one's self and one's soul. So in this case, if your soul is sullied, then any choice you make relating to your work, in theory, will be sullied even if you care deeply about the others involved. See Michael D. Chan's *Aristotle and Hamilton on Commerce and Statesmanship* that covers Aristotle's virtuous guidelines in the ruler-ruled principles on pages 22-25.

5. c
"The correct relationship between a designer and his or her portfolio is one of constant doubt and questioning" as quoted in Adrian Shaughnessy's *How to Be a Graphic Designer Without Losing Your Soul*, 1st edition, page 94. If you answered "*a*" give yourself -2 points for being complacent. If you answered "*d*" stop being a smartass, your website or *iPad are* your portfolio.

6. e
Find enjoyment in all of the steps, not just one or a couple of them. If you answered "*a*" you need to reconsider things, because research is very important, and happy research makes happy design. If you answered "*c*" then what the hell is the matter with you?

7. b
See Jennifer Roback Morse's "Who Is Rational Economic Man?" page 200 in *Self-Interest: Volume 14, part 1*. Also consider what Peter Saville said when he told *The Times* of London in Sept. 15, 2004, "The trouble with graphic design today is: when can you believe it? It's not the message of the designer anymore. Every applied artist ends up selling his or her soul at some point. I haven't done it and look at me. People call me one of the most famous designers in the world and I haven't got any money" (as quoted in *How to Be a Graphic Designer Without Losing Your Soul* 2nd edition, page 25). If you answered "*d*" then calm down and use less exclamation points to achieve greater bliss because yelling is neither blissful nor cool.

8. c
One's personal reasoning steers their creative and financial choices, as does one's culture. When considering Aristotle's virtuous guidelines in the ruler-ruled principles, personal reasons are closer to one's soul (*Ibid* Chan). For a contrasting

view of why clients choose studios, see Adrian Shaughnessy's *How to Be a Graphic Designer Without Losing Your Soul*, 2nd edition, pages 53-54.

9. g
As Paul Rand so eloquently put it in his Nov. 14, 1996 interview with John Maeda, "Design, just as art, has multiple definitions, there is no single definition. Design can be art. Design can be aesthetics. Design is so simple, that's why it is so complicated" (http://www.paulrand.com/foundation/thoughts_maedaMedia/). Furthermore, if you consider advertising and/or marketing to not be included in what you do, read David Ogilvy's *Confessions of an Advertising Man* and *The Unpublished David Ogilvy* as well as *Hey Whipple, Squeeze This* by Luke Sullivan. For thoughts on the kind of work you do and whether it's "good" or "evil" read Milton Glaser's *The Road to Hell* available as part of his *Ambiguity & Truth* essay online (http://www.miltonglaser.com/files/Essays-Ambiguity-8192.pdf).

10. f
Jean Baudrillard's Selected Writings as edited by Mark Poster covers "A universal code: social standing" on pages 19–21, including the absurd notion that "There is no social responsibility without a Rolex watch!" While objects may demand respect, and expensive objects may project a higher status, what did you really have to do in order to earn those expensive objects? Plus, who's really in graphic design for pride?

11. e
Give yourself -5 points if you answered "g" because you are a fucking liar, and we all have bad days. And if you do see any part of design as a "worst" or "set of worsts" or if you dislike the people it involves you with, then you may want to consider another line of work. For insight into defeating "monsters" that get in the way of client work see (magazine) *id29*'s *Slay the Scary Monsters* (http://slaythescarymonsters.com/). For fitness and exercise tips, see "Everything You Know About Fitness Is a Lie" (http://www.mensjournal.com/magazine/everything-you-know-about-fitness-is-a-lie-20120504) or if you purchase the treadmill desk to get off your butt (http://www.amazon.com/TrekDesk-Treadmill-Desks-TD-01-Desk/dp/B002IYRBI0) be sure to read the BBC's report first (http://www.bbc.co.uk/news/magazine-21076461). If you see technology (ancient, modern, or otherwise) as an impediment to enlightenment, read Richard Rojcewicz's *The Gods and Technology: A Reading of Heidegger*, SUNY Press, for deeper insight,

12. b
Steering clear of the competition is normal. For an analogous interpretation of this, See Otfried Hoffe's *Kant's Cosmopolitan Theory of Law and Peace*, Cambridge University Press, page 173, where Hoffe interprets Kant's notion that states could never operate with enlightened self-interest when stronger states would, in theory, take advantage of weaker ones. Give yourself -2 points if you answered "*c*" and stop being so fucking haughty.

13. b
As Spock said, "the needs of the many outweigh the needs of the few" (*Star Trek 2: the Wrath of Khan*, 1982). You can always look for other work. No need to settle on one choice that benefits a minority, but may hurt a majority. And yet, does one have a moral obligation to perform an act if one is capable? What if one's circumstances and responsibility to others *require* that act to be performed, so that those within their responsibility matrix (children, spouse, pets) can carry on their lives, or sustain a living condition they're used to? If you picked "*a*" don't feel bad, then go watch *Breaking Bad* seasons 1–3, paying special attention to season 3 episodes 1–7 for Walter White's perspective on supporting loved ones. R. Kevin Hill's *Nietzsche's Critiques: The Kantian Foundations of His Thought*, Oxford University Press, 2003 pages 198–200, proposes the notion that rational action with enlightened self-interest makes morality, as viewed through Kant's lens, impossible. Also, never have one client that makes up 80% or more of your revenue.

14. e
If you answered "*d*" then you're too optimistic and too much of a control freak, so give yourself -5 points. In *The Handbook of Mass Media Ethics*, edited by Lee Wilkins and Clifford G. Christians, Sherry Baker delves into how enlightened self-interest makes certain assumptions about the outcome of a business relationship (in this case, designer to client). In her article, "The Ethics of Advocacy: Moral Reasoning in the Practice of Public Relations" Baker posits that if neither party was rewarded, then the action was not justified.

Score Key
Less-Than-Zero to 0—*Bitter & Soulless*
1 to 8—*Good & Normal*
9 to 11—*Enlightened*
12 to 13—*Morally Enlightened*
14—*Angelic*

Contributors biographies

The people behind this issue.

Kevin Finn is founder, editor and designer of *Open Manifesto*. Kevin is also founder of *DESIGNerd* an educuational brand dedicated to design enthusiasts. *DESIGNerd 100+* is the first graphic design trivia game in the world, featuring questions from some of the most significant designers, including Stefan Sagmeister, Steven Heller and Lita Talarico.

Kevin also runs his independent design practice TheSumOf. He is Design Consultant to *de Bono Global*, Edward de Bono's global management company. Kevin worked closely with de Bono Global's CEO to brand Edward de Bono's life's work, the first time this has ever been done. Kevin sits on the *de Bono Global* advisory board. He is also Design Associate to *Business Models Inc.*

Andrew Barnum is a designer, educator and songwriter, academic leader, course author, lecturer, workshop facilitator and artist. Andrew works in consultancy with emphasis on User-centred Economy and Social Design Action.

Andrew has been at the forefront of design since the mid-1970s, in Australia and the USA. He has sustained a portfolio career across aspects of the Creative Industry as practitioner, educator and theorist. Andrew completed a Masters by Research from UTS:FASS (2010). His thesis title: *"Re-defining creativity, with particular reference to its sustainability, within the context of the Creative Industry discourse."*

Andrew is currently undertaking Ph.D study at UTS:FASS: *"Song of Place: Locating authentic, contemporary Australian Song-writing practice and its subsequent expression of Australian Cultural Identity and Locality, within the Connected Age of Music 2.0."*

Damian Borchok: In 2014, Damian decided to put his career where his mouth was and resigned after seven years as CEO of *Interbrand* Australia. *For The People* represented a fresh start in helping leaders reimagine business for the 21st Century.

Damian has had an eclectic worklife, having worked in retailing, banking and for a winery, before spending the last 15 years consulting on brand strategy and business transformation, innovation and culture change.

Damian's previous work includes: brand transformations for *Telstra, Alzheimer's Australia* and *SKY TV NZ*; placemaking programs for *The Rocks* and *Darling Harbour*; and cultural projects for the *Sydney Opera House, Opera Australia* and *Griffin Theatre Company*.

Previously a board member of the *Griffin Theatre Company*, Damian is now a board director of the *Australian Design Centre*.

Dr. Edward de Bono is regarded by many as the leading authority in conceptual and creative thinking and the direct teaching of thinking as a skill. The appeal of his work is its simplicity, practicality and universality—the de Bono methods are simple, practical and powerful. They have been used equally by four year-olds and by top executives of some of the world's largest corporations, by young people with Down's Syndrome and Nobel Laureates, to deliver powerful results.

Born in Malta, Dr. Edward de Bono received his initial education at St Edward's College, Malta, and the Royal University of Malta, where he obtained a degree in medicine. Following this, he then proceeded as a Rhodes Scholar to Christchurch, Oxford, where he gained an honors degree in psychology and physiology and then a D.Phil. in medicine. He holds a Phd from Cambridge, a DDes from the Royal Melbourne Institute of Technology, and a LLD from Dundee. He has had faculty appointments at the universities of Oxford, Cambridge, London and Harvard and has been hailed as one of the 250 people who have contributed most to mankind.

Dr. Edward de Bono's entry into the subject of thinking came directly from his early work in medicine with the more complicated interactive systems of the body (glands, kidneys, respiration and circulatory systems) and the need to develop concepts of self-organising information systems. This led to the consideration of behavior in neural networks, (see his book *The Mechanism of Mind*) and his interest in creative thinking and the development of processes for lateral thinking.

Based on his early research into understanding how the brain works as a self-organising information system, Dr. Edward de Bono designed various frameworks and methods of thinking to broaden and maximize the cognitive, conceptual and creative process. As such, much of his work has been of pivotal influence in the explosion around thinking and creativity and innovation in the last forty years.

De Bono originated many of the concepts and frameworks that are widely used today; *Lateral Thinking*—which now has an entry in the Oxford English Dictionary and *Parallel Thinking*®, he is equally renowned for his development of the *Six Thinking Hats*® technique, the *CoRT Thinking Programme*® and the *Direct Attention Thinking Tools (DATT)*® framework.

He has written over 70 books and programmes, with translations into 43 languages, has been invited to lecture in 58 countries and has made three television series.

Dr. de Bono's instruction has been sought by governments, not-for-profit organisations and many of the leading corporations in the world, such as *IBM, Boeing, BT* (UK), *Nokia* (Finland), *Mondadori* (Italy), *Siemens* (Germany), *3M* (Germany), *NTT* (Japan), *GM, Kraft, Nestle, Du Pont, Prudential, Shell, Bosch* (Germany), *Goldman Sachs, Ernst & Young* and many others. One of the leading consultancy companies, *Accenture*, chose him as one of the fifty most influential business thinkers today.

Daniel Everett is an American author and academic best known for his study of the Amazon Basin's Pirahã people and their language. As of July 1, 2010 he serves as Dean of Arts and Sciences at Bentley University in Waltham, Massachusetts. Prior to Bentley University, Everett was Chair of the Department of Languages, Literatures and Cultures at Illinois State University in Normal, Illinois. He has taught at the University of Manchester and is former Chair of the Linguistics Department of the University of Pittsburgh.

Adam Grant is Wharton Business School's youngest full professor and top-rated teacher. He has been recognized as one of *HR* magazine's most influential international thinkers, *BusinessWeek*'s favourite professors, and the world's top 40 business professors under 40. He is the author of *Give and Take*, a *New York Times* bestselling book that has been translated into 27 languages and has been named one of the best books of 2013 by *Amazon*, the *Financial Times*, and the *Wall Street Journal*—as well as one of *Oprah*'s riveting reads, *Harvard Business Review*'s ideas that shaped management, and the *Washington Post*'s books every leader should read. Malcolm Gladwell recently identified Adam as one of his favorite social science writers, calling his work "brilliant."

Stephanie Akkaoui Hughes is founder and lead architect of AKKA Architects (www.akkaarchitects.com). Stephanie is part of a new breed of young visionary architects, who operate beyond the current—and restrained—realm of architecture. A strong advocate of creating value through cross-disciplinary interactions, Stephanie believes that sustainable innovation emerges at the intersection of different forms of interaction.

Stephanie was awarded her professional degree in Architecture with high honours at the American University of Beirut, where she won numerous academic and national awards and competitions. Soon after, she accepted an offer to work at the world renowned architecture practice OMA. During her five years at OMA, Stephanie developed extensive experience around all the phases of large scale architectural and urban projects by engaging in three major projects for the *Qatar Foundation* from the very start until construction: the *Qatar Foundation Headquarters*, the *Strategic Studies Center* and Qatar's *National Library*.

After five years at OMA, Stephanie founded AKKA, an architecture firm which specialises in creating spaces that foster human interaction. AKKA is driven by the vision of *Architecting Interaction©* which explores how can we design contexts that foster human interaction in its different forms, including collaboration, learning, creativity and innovation. Specifically developed to implement the vision of Architecting Interaction, AKKA's process is a collaborative process, based on the communal creation of knowledge. Through the four phases of Understanding, Envisioning, Creating and Adapting, AKKA's team engages in an ongoing consultation with every project's community. At the heart of AKKA lies the dedication to innovate human interactions.

Stephanie is regularly invited to speak and lead workshops at universities, conferences and summits around Europe and the Middle East, among others. On December 1st 2012, Stephanie presented Architecting Interaction at TEDxBelfast.

Ji Lee has an extensive and entrepreneurial career across design and design thinking. Ji is the Creative Lead at Facebook, and former Creative Director at *Google Creative Lab*. Prior to this, he was Creative Director at Droga5 and Art Director at Saatchi & Saatchi. He is known for his personal illustrations (*Time Magazine/The New*

York Times) and has exhibited at Museum of Art and Design (MAD), New York. Fast Company lists Ji as one of America's 50 most influential designers.

He is widely known for his subversive and humorous *Bubble Project*, where he printed stickers resembling comic strip speech bubbles and posted them anonymously on advertisements throughout New York City. This created an unprecedented and live dialogue with the New York public where anyone could write their comments and thoughts in the speech bubbles. Following major media coverage, in 2006, Lee wrote the book, *"Talk Back: The Bubble Project"* which documents the project.

Born in Seoul, South Korea, Lee moved to Brazil when he was 10, and later went to New York City to study at Parsons School of Design. He graduated with a degree in Communication and Graphic Design.

Anne Miltenburg: Since obtaining her BA in Visual Communication from the *Royal Academy of Fine Arts* in 2000, Anne has taken on various roles in the design world: as a designer at *Studio Dumbar*, creative strategist at *Lava*, creative director at *Interbrand*, and since 2012 as an independent brand developer.

Helen Palmer has worked within and for theatres, arts organisations and festivals across the UK for approaching 20 years. She was part of the team that set up and delivered *Cultureshock* (Commonwealth Games North West Cultural Programme), the inaugural *Manchester International Festival* and the Marketing Co-ordination Unit at Marketing Manchester.

Helen is also Director of *Creative Tourist*, a publishing, events and communications agency. *Creative Tourist* specialises in cultural tourism and digital communications, publishing an award-winning online magazine, while also staging cultural events.

Creative Tourist develops intelligent communications strategies that enable organisations and destinations to position themselves as places that cultural tourists actively want to visit. To put it another way, *Creative Tourist* bridges the gap between culture, tourism and the consumer.

Jason Tselentis is a designer, writer, and educator living in North Carolina. He has completed print and interactive design for the Experience Music Project and Science Fiction Museum Hall of Fame, the National Park Service, Continental Tires, and 20th Century Fox. He has also consulted award-winning creative agencies on best practices, and participated in think tanks and research studies with Intel Labs. As Associate Professor at Winthrop University's Department of Design, he teaches visual communication design, brand strategy and development, web design, and typography. Jason has volunteered as Development Director for the Charlotte AIGA, and has served on their Advisory Board since 2009 focusing on education and membership.

His writings about design and visual culture have appeared in Arcade, Eye, mental_floss, Open Manifesto, Print, and HOW magazines. His book *Type, Form & Function* explores typography fundamentals for the novice to advanced designer. Typography Referenced, co-authored with leading educators and professionals from around the world, covers nearly every aspect of typography and lettering including history and contemporary usage, and was named in the 2013 *Outstanding Reference Sources List* by the American Library Association's Reference & User Services Association. The Graphic Designer's Electronic-Media Manual demonstrates how web design principles and practices relate to visual basics that many designers already know.

Between 2003 and 2009 he regularly contributed to the award-winning design forum *Speak Up* as an author. He blogs for RockPaperInk, HOW design, Print, and AIGA.

Back issues

Information on previous issues.

Issue #6: Myth
Very limited stock available.
295 pages.

Open Manifesto #6:
Myth

Available in very limited numbers. Contributors to issue #6 include: *Warren Berger, Andy Chen, Nils Clauss. George Lois, David Mellonie, Anne Miltenburg, Dean Poole, Pepi Ronalds, Allan Savory, Jason Tselentis, Hellen Walters* and *Tom Zoellner.* Their biographies can be found on *www.openmanifesto.net.*

Overview:
Among others, investigative journalist and author **Tom Zoellner** explores the role of the myth in society, focussing on how DeBeers' advertising and marketing infiltrated Japanese culture and seduced the world with diamonds. The legendary **George Lois** talks about his politics, discusses his unique relationship with Esquire editor Harold Hayes, reveals how Paul Rand influenced Bill Bernbach and debunks the Mad Men TV series. **Dean Poole** shares his experiences transitioning from artist to internationally acclaimed designer, discusses the business of design and the influence design has on culture. **Warren Berger** presents an in-depth exploration of the power of Design Thinking, while **Helen Walters** questions the potency of the Design Thinking trend. **Allan Savory** dissects the myths around fossil fuels and climate change, arguing that agriculture has just as much impact on the environment—if not more—ridicules the notion of sustainable projects, shares his views on vertical farming and offers a solution that could possibly save the planet.

Where can I get a copy?
Limited printed stock of *Open Manifesto #6* is available online at www.openmanifesto.net.
Open Manifesto #6 is also available as an ebook online at www.openmanifesto.net.

Details:
295 pages
154mm width x 215mm height / 0.6kg weight
Printed in one colour

Issue #5: Identity
Very limited stock available.
293 pages.

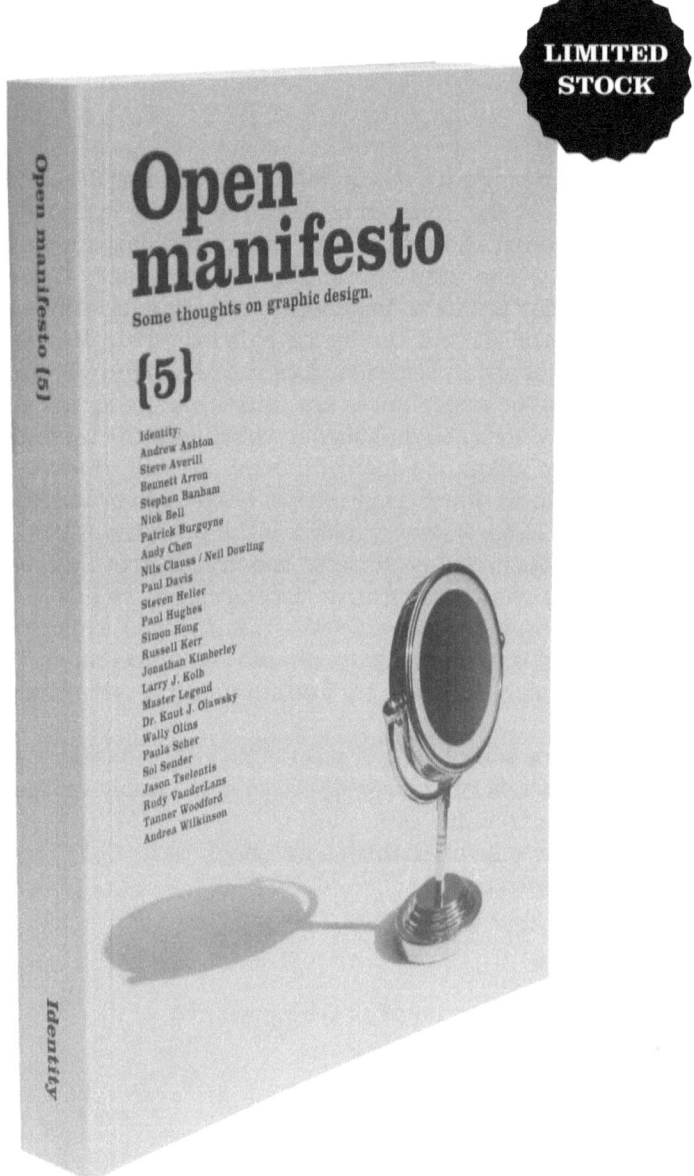

Open Manifesto #5:
Identity

Available in very limited numbers. Contributors to issue #5 include: *Andrew Ashton, Steve Averill, Bennett Arron, Stephen Banham, Nick Bell, Patrick Burgoyne, Andy Chen, Nils Claus/Neil Dowling, Paul Davis, Steven Heller, Paul Hughes, Simon Hong, Russell Kerr, Jonathon Kimberley, Larry J. Kolb, Master Legend, Dr, Knut J. Olawsky, Wally Olins, Paula Scher, Sol Senders, Jason Tselentis, Rudy VanderLans, Tanner Woodford* and *Andrea Wilkinson*. Their biographies can be found on *www.openmanifesto.net*.

Overview:
Among others, **Steve Averill** discusses how he came up with the name *U2* and how his close relationship and design partnership with the Irish rock legends has continued to develop for over 30 years. **Wally Olins** shares his views on the principles behind branding, its impact on society and how we all seek to belong. **Paula Scher** critiques the branding of *New York* and *New York City*, while **Simon Hong** talks about his experiences branding *Abu Dhabi*. **Neil Dowling** and **Nils Clauss** meet with North Korean refugees to discuss the severe challenges they face after escaping to South Korea. **Bennett Arron** talks humorously about identity theft: the theft of his personal identity and his fight to regain it. Real-life Superhero **Master Legend** discusses managing his secret identity, while **Larry J. Kolb** shares his experiences as a *CIA* operative working in the covert world of spies.

Where can I get a copy?
Limited printed stock of *Open Manifesto #5* is available online at www.openmanifesto.net.

Details:
293 pages
154mm width x 215mm height / 0.6kg weight
Printed in one colour

Issue #4: Propaganda
Very limited stock available.
268 pages.

Open Manifesto #4:
Propaganda

Available in very limited numbers. Contributors to issue #4 include: *Vincent Brossel/Reporters Without Borders, Noam Chomsky, Alain de Botton, Paul Davis, Chris Doyle, Milton Glaser, Mark Gowing, Jacqueline Hill, Steven Heller, Katherine Hepworth, Alya Karime, Errol Morris, Julia Park, Nurit Peled-Elhanan, David Pidgeon, Peter Saville, David Stairs, Elizabeth (Dori) Tunstall* and *Alex Tyers.* Their biographies can be found on *www.openmanifesto.net.*

Overview:
Among others, **Peter Saville** discusses his views on the evolution of the graphic design industry and also questions the role of truth in branding. **Errol Morris** examines how images can be taken out of context on a regular basis and used for propagandistic ends. **Noam Chomsky** looks at the relationship between entertainment and propaganda and offers some advice on how to read between the lines of daily information. **Milton Glaser** talks about the importance of dissent, while **Nurit Peled-Elhanan** takes a look at the Israeli education system of anti-Palestinian indoctrination. **Jacqueline Hill** takes us on a journey through the ancient history of branding and how it has been continually used in propagandistic ways right up to the present day, and **Katherine Hepworth** looks at the motivations behind *Brand Australia.* **Paul Davis** presents us with thirteen despots while **Alain de Botton** goes against the grain by offering a convincing case for the possibility of *good propaganda.*

Where can I get a copy?
Limited printed stock of *Open Manifesto #4* is available online at www.openmanifesto.net.

Details:
268 pages
154mm width x 215mm height / 0.5kg weight
Printed in one colour

Issue #3: What is graphic design?
Very limited stock available.
229 pages.

Open Manifesto #3:
What is Graphic Design?

Available in very limited numbers. Contributors to issue #3 include:: *Andrew Ashton, Andrew Barnum, Mark Braddock, Andrew Breitenberg, Craig Bremner, Zoé Barber, Robert Cook, Paul Davis, Rami Elhanan, Bob Gill, George Hardie, Anthony Inciong, David Lancashire, Harmine Louwe, Quentin Newark, Simon Pemberton, Tim Ritchie, Brian Stapleton, Jason Tselentis, David Throsby* and *Alex Tyers*. Their biographies can be found on *www.openmanifesto.net*.

Overview:
George Hardie discusses illustration, teaching, technology and the nuances of cultural exchange. *Rami Elhanan* talks about the Israeli/Palestinian issue and the importance of integrity, forgiveness and clear communication. *Professor David Throsby* looks at national identity, multiculturalism and the economic significance design has on society. *Bob Gill* proves there is always more than one solution to a problem, while *Zoë Barber* addresses the *Ego* in design. *Andrew Ashton* takes a close look at graphic design in Australia and *Robert Cook* sits with *Mark Braddock* and asks what graphic design is really all about.

Where can I get a copy?
Limited printed stock of *Open Manifesto #3* is available online at www.openmanifesto.net.

Details:
229 pages
154mm width x 215mm height / 0.6kg weight
Printed in one colour

Issue #2: Interpreting Visual Language.
Sold out.
182 pages.

Open Manifesto #2:
Interpreting visual language

SOLD OUT

Contributors to the second issue include: *Stephen Banham, Andrew Barnum, Lissa Barnum, Craig Bremner, Anthony Cahalan, Glenn Churches, Daniel Mudie Cunningham, Edward de Bono, Ross Gibson, Corinne Goode, Ingvar Kenne, Katherine Moline, Ros Moriarty, Stefan Sagmeister, Ebany Spencer* and *Narelle Vine.* Their biographies can be found on *www.openmanifesto.net.*

Overview:
Among others, **Edward de Bono** discusses the power of visual language and the immediacy it provides over verbal language, how the brain organises visual patterns and why he chooses to draw as he speaks when delivering a presentation. **Ros Moriariy** explains how enduring knowledge about preserving the (Australian) continent, for maybe 10,000 years, was enshrined in the symbols of Aboriginal visual language, handed down through both ceremony and daily life. **Stefan Sagmeister** debunks his previous *Style=Fart* motto, shares his views on globalisation, talks about his earlier aspirations to be a musician or film director, discusses his first year without clients and offers his comments on Australian design. **Ingvar Kenne** talks about the universality of *the image* as a means of communication, discusses his difficulty in getting clients to use Aboriginal models in fashion shoots and offers his views on the rise of digital photography, while **Andrew Barnum** asks **Professor Ross Gibson** whether there an Australian graphic tradition, discusses how design feeds into national identity and talks about the opportunism involved in the appropriation of Indigenous culture without proper context.

Where can I get a copy?
Open Manifesto #2 (Print) is sold out and not available for purchase.
Open Manifesto #2 is available as an ebook online at www.openmanifesto.net.

Issue #1: Given the chance, what would you say?
Very limited stock available.
101 pages.

**Open Manifesto #1:
Given the chance what would you say?**

Available in very limited numbers. Contributors to the first issue include: *Craig Bremner, Émilie de Comarmond, Nicole Foreshew, Vince Frost, Mary Gallagher, Robyn Gower, Hina Qureshi* and *David Terrazas.* Their biographies can be found on *www.openmanifesto.net*.

Overview:
In the wake of September 11, **Hina Qureshi** discusses the difficulties of being Muslim today, while exploring her Arabic design heritage and her desire to build a bridge between Western and Middle Eastern communities through design. **Vince Frost** talks about his passion for design and his interest in demystifying the design process for the general public, the state of design education and the pros and cons of the *First Things First 2000 Manifesto.* **Craig Bremner** addresses young designers with an open letter stressing the importance of design history and theory, the rise of the celebrity designer (and the issues therein) and reminds students that they cannot erase themselves from the work they produce—that something of their character, beliefs, values, etc, will be visible. **Mary Gallagher** critiques the tabloidization of mass media, including the cultural function of media scandals, arguing that these trends can empower the lower classes as social agents. And **Nicole Foreshew,** a young Aboriginal designer, shares her personal journey in using art and design to highlight the connections between spirituality and the land, while also seeking deeper and more informed ways to present Indigenous culture to a wider audience.

Where can I get a copy?
Open Manifesto #1 (Print) is sold out and not available for purchase.

Thanks

Acknowledgments by Kevin Finn

As always, the contributors have my deepest gratitude—for their generosity, thoughts, words, general enlightenment, images and opinions. But most of all, for their patience.

Sincere thanks to my wife, Keren, and my Dad for his continued support and encouragement with every issue of *Open Manifesto*. I still find it difficult to put into words just how much this means to me.

Special thanks to my friend and colleague KT Doyle, for her copy-proofing, general advice, suggestions and unwavering support. Her input is immensely appreciated.

Finally, but by no means least, I would like to extend a special thanks to you, the reader, without whom this publication would have little purpose. I hope *Open Manifesto* encourages you in some way, and at some level, regardless of your profession or position, to discuss the wider issues relating to the design professions and design culture today.

As always, you are the reason for *Open Manifesto*.

Thank you.

Kevin Finn

Open manifesto.

www.ingramcontent.com/pod-product-compliance
Lightning Source LLC
Chambersburg PA
CBHW022004160426
43197CB00007B/266